escape FROM
CHURCH, INC.

escape FROM
CHURCH, INC.

The Return of the Pastor-Shepherd

E. GLENN WAGNER
with Steve Halliday

ZondervanPublishingHouse
Grand Rapids, Michigan

A Division of HarperCollinsPublishers

Escape from Church, Inc.
Copyright © 1999 by E. Glenn Wagner

Requests for information should be addressed to:

 Zondervan Publishing House
Grand Rapids, Michigan 49530

Library of Congress Cataloging-in-Publication Data

Wagner, E. Glenn.
    Escape from Church, Inc.: the return of the pastor-shepherd / Glenn Wagner
with Steven Halliday.
    p. cm.
    Includes bibliographical references.
    ISBN: 0–310–22888–3
    1. Pastoral theology I. Halliday, Steve, 1957- . II. Title.
BV4011.W28 1999
253—dc21

                             99–30792
                               CIP

This edition printed on acid-free paper.

Published in association with the literary agency of Alive Communications, Inc., 1465 Kelly Johnson Blvd. #320, Colorado Springs, CO 80920.

Interior design by Laura Klynstra

Printed in the United States of America

99 00 01 02 03 04 / ❖ DC / 10 9 8 7 6 5 4 3 2 1

....

DEDICATION

....

To: God's Shepherds

CONTENTS

INTRODUCTION:
WHY I WROTE THIS BOOK

How do we bring men and women into an ever-deepening relationship with God and with one another in the body of Christ? That question has consumed me for many years now. I have believed for a long time that Christians yearn for the kind of relationships they see in the Scriptures, but they don't know how to develop them.

This conviction grew stronger during my time as a vice president with Promise Keepers. The very first PK conference drew four thousand men to the Coors Events Center at the University of Colorado in Boulder. I was amazed to see what happened. The men there went "deep" really fast. Many even opened up to their need for Christ on the basis of a simple testimony from Coach McCartney and an even simpler invitation from Randy Phillips, in which he said, "Listen, guys. We're not going to do anything fancy. Let me ask you to be a man. If you need Jesus, come down front." That was pretty much it—and hundreds of men poured down front. Soon the rest of the audience gave a spontaneous standing ovation in which the applause went on, it seemed, forever. I had never seen anything like it. Men were crying as others went forward to receive Christ. I wasn't prepared for the "heart hunger" I saw.

And it didn't stop with Boulder. Wherever I traveled around the country after that, I saw the same phenomenon. Guys let down barriers, dismantled walls, wept with one another—and they kept telling me they had never experienced such a thing or tasted such relationships in their home churches.

Promise Keepers convinced me that both men and women desire strong relationships; they want the reality that comes only through person-to-person contact. But current church structures often frustrate their desires.

Now, don't get me wrong. I love the church. I don't just *like* the church; I *love* it. I took a brief break from pastoral ministry to be involved full-time with Promise Keepers, but I always knew that I would return to the pastorate. I am called to be a pastor, and I willingly give my life on behalf of the church.

But I'm also concerned that the church is not making the impact it was created to have. I'm concerned about the growing numbers of "dropout Christians" who have been hurt and abused in churches that seem to see people as objects to be used for some grander scheme. I'm concerned about our high rate of pastoral burnout and the numbers of pastors being dismissed because they don't fit the corporate model now in vogue.

In the United States we do things so big that we give ourselves the illusion of success. But all statistics show that North America is the only continent where the church is not growing; it's not even keeping pace with population growth. America is the second highest missionary-receiving nation in the world. On a per capita basis, Ireland sends out more missionaries per year than we do.[1]

You may look at those statistics and ask, "With everything we have, with the millions of dollars that we spend, *why aren't we going someplace?*" I firmly believe it's because we have bought into gimmicks and programs—the razzle-dazzle, Las Vegas syndrome of Christianity, all flash and lights and gaudiness. But we have forgotten the basics of what it means to be the church and do ministry.

My tenure at Promise Keepers helped me to pinpoint some of the specific problems, but the red light began to go off in my head long before that.

For many years I had struggled with the question, *How do we do church?* I went to all the seminars, just like everyone else. I attended How to Be a Better Manager, How to Do Strategic Planning, How to Lead, How to Grow a Church, *ad infinitum.* I read hundreds of books on church growth and leadership development, both Christian and secular. And all the while I tried to analyze my frustrations with ministry. Certainly I had enjoyed some successes, but I also sensed that there had to be more than just buying the latest, hottest program.

During this time I helped found the Seminary of the East, where we developed our curriculum on a relational style of ministry preparation. The idea was to pair every student with a pastor and a lay mentor, whose input formed a portion of the student's grade. Suppose, for example, that a student was studying the book of Romans. With faculty and mentor involvement, the student would design two learning contracts, one relating to a ministry skill in the local church, another to an area of personal character development—say, on prayer or fasting. We wanted our students to mature not only intellectually but also in their hearts and lives. We wanted them to experience vital relationships. We hoped that as students walked through this process, they would so fall in love with it that they would practice the model for the rest of their ministries. They would always be in accountable relationships; they would always bring others into relationship, rather than just doing their gig and running their programs. We focused on the New Testament's "one another" emphasis that most pastors never get. Still, I continued to wrestle with the question, *What does it look like to be the church?*

My perspective began to crystallize at Promise Keepers when we started to put together training material on how to equip a church to reach men. We developed a philosophy of ministry that pushed against the task orientation that drives most men. We had found that if a church had any kind of men's ministry, it probably revolved around tasks rather than relationships. Yet men grow through relationships, not tasks.

So when we began teaching these relational principles to pastors, we immediately ran into trouble. The pastors' entire orientation and training had been, "Here's how you run a program." I kept talking to pastors who said, "I know how to buy a curriculum. But how do I structure my church so that I can bring men into an ever-deepening relationship with God and one another in the body of Christ?" They were used to running a twelve-week discipleship series— and *voilà*, at the end of twelve weeks, the guy was discipled. Or maybe it took a year and a half to go through the curriculum; *then* the guy was a disciple. Yet the Scriptures talk continually about relationship. Deuteronomy 6:7, for example, tells us to teach our children when we walk along the way, when we lie down, and when we rise up. Jesus taught his disciples through relationship.

Finally it dawned on me that the issue was not so much what pastors were doing but how they were thinking. Because they didn't *think* right, they couldn't *do* right. We had to go back to the basics.

This book is born out of a passion for the church and a deep commitment to what I believe is God's chosen model for successful pastors and churches. We don't need to look to sociological or psychological or managerial experts to tell us how to make the church "work." We need only to follow what God already has told us in his Word: Shepherd the flock of God! This book attempts to unpack what that means.

ACKNOWLEDGMENTS

As "iron sharpens iron" has been the story of this book. The ministry staff and elders of Calvary Church encouraged me to teach and live the Shepherd's model. Rick Christian and Jeff Tikson believed in the message; Steve Halliday and Larry Libby gave shape to my words and thoughts; my assistant, Bev Modzell, helped me find the time to complete the manuscript; and my family—Susan, Haven, and Justin—gave up some time with husband and father. I love and appreciate each one of you.

Part 1

LIKE SHEEP WITHOUT A SHEPHERD

Chapter 1

THE CHURCH, INC.

A subtle heresy has crept into the evangelical church. It seemed innocent enough at first, since it came from people who love Jesus Christ and his church. These folks meant well and sincerely wanted to stem the tide that has been threatening to engulf us.

But the end is worse than the beginning.

The problem? Like Esau, we pastors have sold our biblical birthright as shepherds called by God for the pottage of skills and gimmicks designed by humans. We have misunderstood the role of pastor and defined it incorrectly. We have left our biblical and theological moorings.

The result? Our churches are struggling mightily, Christians are wandering from the faith, and pastors are burning out at alarming rates. That troubles me greatly because I love the church. I passionately believe in the body of Christ—yet I think it's in deep trouble.

Now, don't get me wrong. I don't believe the church is dying and ready for burial. Too much good is happening, especially around the world, to make such a rash statement. I trust the Lord Jesus, and he said, "I will build my church, and the gates of Hades will not overcome it" (Matthew 16:18). I believe his words with all my heart. Jesus intends to conquer for the kingdom.

I also believe Satan understands that he cannot and will not overcome the church—*but he will cripple it if he can.* And believe it or not, we seem to be helping him do just that. Let me explain what I mean.

LOSS OF INFLUENCE

No matter how you look at the statistics, they seem to point to the same conclusion: The American church exerts precious little influence on society. Not only is church growth failing to keep up with the nation's birthrate, but the behavior of those who identify themselves as Christians cannot be distinguished statistically from those who make no such claim.

I have pastored long enough to see firsthand the ever-decreasing impact the American church is having for the things of God. Others have seen this frightening trend for some time.

Pollster and author George Barna has written several books detailing the challenges faced by the modern church. In a recent work he warned, "Despite the activity and chutzpah emanating from thousands of congregations, the Church in America is losing influence and adherents faster than any other major institution in the nation." Then he predicted one of two outcomes for our nation within the next few years: either "massive spiritual revival" or "total moral anarchy."[1] It all depends, he said, on whether the church can rouse itself to respond to current trends.

A PLETHORA OF ANSWERS (THAT HAVEN'T WORKED)

Over the years many "experts" and consultants have suggested a dizzying variety of cures for the church's malaise. They spoke, and we rushed out to buy their books and attend their seminars that so confidently promised to lead us into an era of unprecedented success and growth—

the pastoral promised land. Strangely, even as the American church declined, the number of resources designed to make us more effective as pastors and to help our churches increase their impact simply exploded. Today there is no shortage of seminars, books, tapes, conferences, and courses, all produced to equip us to capture a world for Christ. Never before in the history of the church has there been so much available to so many, yet with so little effect.

Not long ago the so-called "experts" (I've always wondered how you get that title) came to us pastors and said, "The best way to get people involved in the ministry of your church is to put them on boards and committees." So we launched countless boards and committees, recruited warm bodies like mad, and nearly wore ourselves out shuffling paper.

A little later a new batch of "experts" came around to insist, "You know what? Your churches are struggling because you pastors don't know about management. You don't know how to manage your congregation. You don't know how to manage the ministry. You don't know how to manage the budgets."

So along came truckloads of books, courses, and seminars on management, and all of us rushed out to read, attend, and devour their wisdom. We kept hearing, "Pastor, if your church is ever going to grow, you must learn some basic management techniques and principles. If you attend these seminars and read these books, you'll be better equipped to develop mission statements, vision statements, and strategic plans."

Of course, the "experts" failed to tell us that the people in the business world from whom they took their theories already knew they didn't work. They had also written big strategic plans . . . and found them useless. They stuck them on a shelf and did nothing with them, except when stockholders wanted to see something impressive on paper.

A few years later these same "experts" (most of whom had never pastored a day in their lives) returned to announce, "Folks, that's really not the way to do it." Of course, they never asked forgiveness for messing things up in the first place. Just once I'd like an "expert" to come back and say, "I gave you some bad advice and I fouled up the church. Please forgive me." But they don't do that. Instead, they pitch yet another seminar and another book, all the while sending those never-ending packs of three-by-five cards that so confidently proclaim, "Do this and your church will double in six months."

At any rate, this batch of "experts" came along to say, "What you really need to do is to involve people in relationships." So we took their courses and seminars, but somehow the church didn't get any better.

That didn't stop these guys. They spun on their heels and declared, "You know what the *real* problem is? You began to learn a little about management, but you're not leaders. There's a vast difference between managers and leaders. Your most critical need is to learn about leadership." So books on leadership began rolling off the presses like lemmings leaping off a cliff.

But still the church kept losing ground.

Let's do a quick recap. First it was bus ministry. Then it was body life. Then it was identifying your market. Then the church unleashed. Then spiritual gifts, personality profiles, cell churches, megachurches, and metachurches. Then seeker services. Then purpose-driven churches.

Most recently it's felt needs, so we try to address every felt need. The problem is, a church can't organize enough ministries to address every felt need. It simply cannot be done—the landscape is littered with felt needs. So pastors come out of conferences saying, "You know, that's really great—but how do I do it with one hundred people? I can't meet that many needs in my community. I can't invite Gary

Smalley to lead a seminar. I can't sponsor this or that. What am I supposed to do?" And so the frustration builds.

Now, no one contests that we have a problem. The multitude of ideas and proposals about how to fix the problem demonstrates that we all know it exists. We continue to hear about this technique or that strategy, everything from better vision statements to strategic planning to organizational retooling to effective leadership principles.

Yet our dismal situation has barely budged. Why, when we have available to us more resources than ever, are we no better at evangelizing the lost and instigating positive change in the church? Please don't get me wrong. It's not that any one of these solutions, in and of itself, is bad. But when they are laid over a wrong pastoral identity in a church functioning with a wrong theological grid, good things soon turn destructive.

It seems to me that everyone has a leash around the pastor's neck except the Lord. Pastors get dragged here and there so much that they soon begin to think that the Bible is irrelevant, that their calling is unimportant, and that they have nothing to say. Because most pastors have never lived in the business world or sat in a corporate board meeting, they start to believe that they cannot have an effective ministry.

I beg to differ.

THE UNDERLYING PROBLEM

I believe that the one problem underlying all others is that we have moved both pastors and churches from a community model to a corporation model. In some churches the pastor is the preaching machine while someone else runs the business side of things. In other churches the pastor is the CEO, the boss, the chairman of the board. But in both cases the pastor is a corporate officer, not a shepherd.

Imagine how frustrating this can be to someone just out of seminary who believes with all his[2] heart that God has called him to enter the pastoral ministry. While he may have tasted only a little of what that means, *pastor* is the image that filled his original vision.

But when he gets to his first church, it's nothing like what he saw in his call. Now he hears, "You have to come up with a six-year strategic plan. You must create and manage the budget. Here is our list of twenty things that the CEO does at this church." And all the while the new pastor is thinking, *But I'm here because I care about people.*

Sooner or later, that frazzled pastor is probably going to shift into the easiest route for ministry. It's tough to beat your head against the wall, as a friend of mine who was planting a church in Spain discovered. Once when I went to visit him, he told me, "Not one of the first twenty-five things we've tried has succeeded. Every one of them has completely failed."

"What are you going to do?" I asked.

"I'm going to keep running against that wall," he declared. "Eventually the wall is going to crack."

About a year and a half later, my friend returned to the United States to pastor an already established church. "Glenn," he explained with weariness in his voice, "that wall is just too thick. I can't get through it. I'm just going to do what I know how to do."

That's one route to pastoral burnout, but there are others. I think of the pastor who really believes that if he gets another one hundred people to attend his church, he will feel better about ministry. So the Lord blesses and another hundred people come—but now he thinks about quitting.

What happened? I've heard numerous pastors say, "There has to be more than creating nice Christian people." That's easy . . . but not terribly fulfilling. You can teach your Bible lessons, do your thing, maintain the status quo. The problem is, somewhere along the line, anyone who is really called by God to be a pastor says, "There has to be more than this."

Called pastors know instinctively that success is not measured by programs. It's not gauged by how many outreach events a church holds. Pastors I know who have left the ministry make comments such as, "I thought there was going to be something more. I thought there would be something else, something eternal. But all I saw was the day-to-day." That's a major reason why pastors change churches, on average, every eighteen months. They tire of pushing against the wall, against ministry forms that seem to keep them from real ministry.

On February 10, 1998, I preached this basic message to four thousand pastors at a Promise Keepers gathering. Boy, did I provoke a lot of conversations and get a ton of mail! One youth pastor ran up and butted right into another discussion I was having. "I received my call to ministry because I believe God has called me to bring people into a deeper relationship with Christ and to go beyond the norms," he said breathlessly. "But my senior pastor keeps telling me to back off and to stop rocking the boat if I want to keep my job, if I want to be a pastor for a long time. But you're telling me to rock the boat even if I lose my job, to become what God has called me to be as a pastor."

"Well, yes," I replied, after recovering from his onslaught, "although I don't want to be blamed for your losing your job and your ministry."

I know far too many pastors who struggle desperately under the pressure to "just run the programs." Somewhere along the line, all of us must decide whether we're going to sell our soul to that corporate model.

One man who decided he just couldn't do that any longer is the Reverend Terry Swicegood, former pastor of the 3,700-member Myers Park Presbyterian Church in Mecklenburg, North Carolina.[3] Swicegood resigned his position as senior minister in January 1999 because, as he told *The Charlotte Observer*, "I'm a guy with a pastor's heart, and I'm being a CEO." In a letter to church members, Swicegood said he yearned to be a pastor, a spiritual leader, a teacher, and a friend—but "as presently constituted, the job of senior minister of Myers Park Presbyterian Church requires long and full days of managing, planning and strategizing." The breaking point for Swicegood came one evening when he looked over a log of his daily activities and realized that he had spent eleven of his fourteen hours of work that day in meetings and planning. He told the *Observer*, "I looked down the road to my future and said, 'This is my future.' I just felt absolutely drained. It was kind of an epiphany."

IT'S NOT JUST PASTORS

Certainly, pastors are burning out left and right. But the case could be made just as strongly that far more congregational members are burning out. They get plugged into the programs, they power the machinery, they come out on the other side ... and they've had enough.

Laypeople are wondering what's going on. It just doesn't *feel* right. Something is missing. The church feels cold, detached. "The pastor talks about family," they say, "but it doesn't feel that way. I really want to believe my church is a family. I need that family around me. I crave it inside. But I walk in and out and never feel touched by a sense of family. Why is that?"

I believe it's because corporate structures can never produce communities. People feel used by corporations, not nurtured by them. Employees of a corporation know their sole purpose is to make someone else rich and successful, so they feel disconnected. Often they feel patronized. They might hear from a superior that "we're a family," but they see families getting downsized left and right and their own family's benefits slashed.

There is precious little loyalty in a corporation. Why? Because it's hard to be loyal to a machine! Could it be that's why so many people these days jump from church to church? They don't feel connected. It's hard to leave a community, but it's not tough at all to leave a corporation.

The fact is, many of our people feel that we've created *The Church, Inc.* During the past few decades we in the church have been busy creating, not communities, but corporations—and there's a vast difference! Consider a few of the contrasts between what is most important in these two distinct models:

Corporation	Community
Programs	People
Product	Purpose
Tasks	Relationships
Controlling	Enabling
Benefits (so employees are productive)	Blessing
Money	Ministry
Employment	Enrichment
Entitlement	Encouragement
Production	Provision
Systems	Salvation
Rules	Relationships
Management	Mentoring
Industry	Investment
Competition	Compassion
Performance	Process
Profits	People
Numbers	Nourishment
Promotion	Preferral (others)
Demands	Dedication
Image	Intimacy
Organization	Organism
Management	Ministry
Bottom Line	Lines of Communication

Do you think my analysis is off base? Then just talk to a few people in the pews. I would be shocked if pretty quickly you didn't hear something like, "I don't sense a family here. I'm carrying all these weights and burdens and my life is falling apart, but I don't know how to get help. I don't know who cares. Does *anybody* care?"

We have Sunday school teachers who think they are around simply to disseminate information, to create a classroom full of knowledge junkies. And they rightly wonder, *Is that all it is? Those with the biggest notebooks and the most colors of ink in their Bibles at the end of life win?*

We have the man in the pew who says, "I was told that this book, this Bible, would revolutionize my life. I've memorized hundreds of verses—but my life is still a mess. Why is it that I can sit in the middle of two thousand people and feel absolutely alone?"

We have the woman who has volunteered for everything. She was told, "If you use your gifts, you'll be fulfilled" . . . but still she feels empty.

When one pastor I know arrived to begin his ministry at a new church, a number of people approached him to plead, "Pastor, go easy on us. We're burned out. We've done all the programs, we've built the buildings, we've raised the money, we've had the biggest programs in town—the biggest Christmas concerts, the biggest Easter extravaganzas, and all the rest. And we're absolutely burned out. What did all of that get us?"

I've talked to scores of people from churches all across the country who seem to be singing the same sad tune. "Glenn," they confess, "we heard this vision, so we built the buildings and raised the money and ran the programs. First we had buses. Then we had small groups. Next we had this or that." They recite the list of every program or strategy or plan their church has tried. They look at me with resignation and despair in their tired eyes and ask, "So what?"

I grieve for these people. I can't tell you how many men and women I have sat with who have raised literally millions of dollars for church buildings and projects but who do not attend church anymore. Why not? Their disillusionment just killed them. They felt terribly used and abused in the process of "building the church."

Obviously, there's something desperately wrong with this picture.

HOW DID WE GET HERE?

I've been pondering this bleak state of affairs for a long time, and I've asked myself and others, "How did we get to this discouraging place? Where did we go astray? How did we end up tying ourselves to a model that sees the church more as a corporation than as a community of faith? When did we start training CEOs rather than pastors?"

First, let me say that there are no villains here (at least no human ones). The "experts" who sold us the programs, methods, and strategies genuinely love the Lord. They really want the church to advance and to thrive. They promote the next big thing, whatever it is, because they love the Lord with all of their hearts. Like the rest of us, they want more than a year-end report that indicates we're in the black.

What do they want? They want the same things that we all want. They are looking for relationships, for connectedness, for a sense of purpose and vision. They want to be "the people of God." They want to live as "one body," with "one Spirit ... one hope ... one Lord, one faith, one baptism; one God and Father of all, who is over all and through all and in all" (Ephesians 4:4–6). In other words, they want the kind of church that the Bible describes. The problem is, I don't think they have always pursued it in the way the Bible directs.

WHOSE VISION SHOULD WE FOLLOW?

Many a parishioner has said, "Pastor, I want to believe in what you're telling us. I want to follow your lead about the direction we need to go. But understand this: I've been at this church forty years, during which time I've been told to go in at least forty different directions. Quite frankly, Pastor, none of them has accomplished a whole lot. We've seen surges of growth, but we've also seen people disappointed and leave. Is there one thing that is true for us forever? Or does it change every time a new pastor comes? Is it really 'new pastor, new vision'? Shouldn't there be one overarching vision for the church? Why does every pastor seem to have a different vision?"

So thoughtful people ask, "What is it that defines us? Where are we supposed to go? And why?" They are understandably frustrated—and some of them are scared stiff their pastor will leave. They simply don't want to go through it all over again!

A joke I heard the other day illustrates this fear. A pastor resigned after finishing an effective ministry. On his last Sunday a member of his congregation was standing at the door, crying her eyes out. "Oh, Pastor," she sobbed, "how will we ever find anyone to replace you?"

"I'm sure the denominational leaders will help you find someone even better than I," he replied reassuringly.

"Oh sure," she said bitterly, "that's what they say every time. But it always gets worse!"

Many church people live under just those kinds of fears. Why? Because the gimmicks and strategies and visions and programs change every time there is a change in leadership.

I want to make it clear that I am not opposed to developing a specific vision for your area, a vision that reflects your community's uniqueness and diversity. But I insist that something permanent, solid, and unchanging must lie at the core of any vision. Our churches will never succeed simply by latching on to every hot new program that comes around.

I fully agree that our churches need visionary leadership, but I think the overarching vision must be the Lord's vision for his people. From what I can tell, it's a pretty simple one—but, oh, how it works!

BACK TO THE BEGINNING

If we go back to the very beginning, back to the Lord's bedrock idea for his people, back to the Bible's fundamental plan for the church, what do we find? We find shepherds and sheep.

In essence, what all the polls tell us about men and women longing for relationships, searching for family, and seeking community, is that people need still waters. They need some green pastures. They need their souls restored. What they really need are shepherds who care about them! They don't want to become lamb chops. And although they don't mind producing wool, they don't want to be fleeced.

People are fed up with the rancher model in which they are tagged, fattened up, butchered, and sold for mutton. No wonder the church isn't working like it should! We have been following one model after another, all of which completely differ from what God sets out in the Scriptures. We've built our churches and our ministry models off of everything but a sound ecclesiology (see chapter 3).

Our Lord didn't design it like that. When God wanted to give his people a picture of the way he wanted them to relate to one another in community, he chose the metaphor of sheep and a shepherd. He did so for a reason. He could have chosen any number of other metaphors to portray the leaders of his people—general, sergeant, king, overlord, director, prophet, patriarch—but he didn't. He chose the shepherd, the human vocation that most closely parallels his own character and his own way of relating to his people.

Could it be that both pastors and churches are struggling because we have lost sight of God's vision for pastoral ministry? Do we need to revive that vision once again?

REVIVAL, YES! BUT TO WHAT?

My wife, Susan, and I have always been passionate about ministry. When we first began in the pastorate, we counted among our friends a group of about ten young couples in ministry. A lot of older people considered us a bunch of naive, idealistic youngsters, but we disregarded their skepticism and pressed ahead, aggressive to do the work of the kingdom.

Unfortunately, times have changed. Today Susan and I grieve that only about half of that group remains passionate about ministry. Most of them simply run their programs. It's comfortable, easy. At some point they made a decision: "I wanted to be a pastor, but the price tag is too high."

One of our friends—one of the few who is still passionate about ministry—pastors a difficult church. If that church doesn't kill him, nothing can. In twenty years, my friend has not lost a bit of his passion to be a shepherd. He leads a church of over a thousand, but he still visits individuals in the congregation. He still gets with them personally and lets them know by his actions that he loves them. He's not merely the guy in the corner office.

Recently my friend confessed, "Glenn, everyone tells me that I have to be a rancher. But I'm a shepherd, not a rancher. So every Thursday, I randomly visit people who are not among the Who's Who of the church. Every week, I go see some of my lesser-known sheep. I keep a list of people who aren't that involved. I seek them out and minister to them because I am a shepherd. I believe that if I love my sheep, this church will grow and produce."

I believe my friend is on to something! If George Barna is right that "the Church in America has no more than five years—perhaps even less—to turn itself around and begin to affect the culture, rather than be affected by it,"[4] then we must do everything in our power to return the church to a biblical understanding of what a pastor does and is. The pastor is not a rancher or a CEO. He is not a general or a king or an admiral. Above all else, the pastor is a shepherd.

I also agree with Barna that, before we can hope to turn the church into the kingdom powerhouse God meant it to be, "we must rekindle our passion for God, recapture a sense of urgency about ministry, and respond strategically to the challenges before us."[5] But how do we do that? How can we best accomplish that critical task?

I am encouraged that many of God's people have seen the trouble in our country and in our churches and have raised their voices to mobilize believers to pray for revival. Even as I write, pastors are gathering to pray for revival like never before during my time in the ministry. They are coming together and crying out to God with other pastors— individuals with whom they would not have exchanged greetings even a short while ago. This combination of spiritual crisis and the moving of God's Spirit is bringing pastors to their knees to seek God's divine intervention. Recognizing the peril of the times, pastors are praying together for revival.

What is revival? Revival is being restored to a former condition. "I was once alive, but now I need to be resuscitated. Someone needs to put those paddles on my chest and zap me back to life!"

As pastors, we are praying and crying out to God for revival. But I cannot help but wonder if we are asking to be revived to a former condition that is not what God intended for us in the first place.

We do not need to revive a structure designed by humans or some gimmick gleaned from the pages of church history. We must not attempt to revive a strategy created for another time and place. What we need is an ancient—but nonetheless radical—answer.

We need shepherds of God's flock who model themselves and their ministries after the Chief Shepherd. When we *first* ask God what *he* thinks our churches need to do in order to become salt and light to a decaying, dark world, then we will be on to something that really works—for everyone. In sum, we need to revive and return to God's original model for pastoral ministry, a model that we have neglected far too long.

Chapter 2

THE NEGLECTED MODEL

I had heard about this book long before I finally managed to track it down. It sounded so relevant, so incisive, so needed—so dead-on, knock-me-down true. Yet it remained so elusive. For years I could lay my hands only on tantalizing tidbits of its full message, like the enticing words of Warren Wiersbe, then senior pastor of Moody Memorial Church in Chicago, words that had been photocopied from the foreword to a 1973 reissue of this rare book:

> This book is one of perhaps a dozen in my library that I try to read again each year. It does my heart good! It reminds me of my privileges and responsibilities as one of God's shepherds, and it makes me want to do a better job of preaching the Word and pastoring my flock. And it always convicts me!
>
> We are being told these days that the church is dying, that we must get a "new look" or a "new message" or that we will disappear completely. Without closing his eyes to the changes around him, Jefferson [the author of the book] goes straight to the Bible for the answer: *let the preacher be a pastor and the flock will strengthen itself and*

increase. No gimmicks, nothing spectacular: simply a dedicated man of God going in and going out among his people with the refreshing Word of life.

These lectures were delivered in 1912, but there is a freshness and relevance about them because they are based on the unchanging Word of God. Human nature has not changed! Now, as then, our cities are teeming with people who are as "sheep not having a shepherd." The growing isolation and loneliness of modern society present a great opportunity for the pastor who has a shepherd's heart.

May the Great Shepherd of the sheep give us grace to be faithful under-shepherds, to seek the lost sheep, to lead and feed the flock, to nurture the precious lambs, to protect them from the wolves, and to help them mature to the glory of God.

Charles Edward Jefferson, the author of the elusive book Wiersbe so effectively lauds, served as pastor of the famed Broadway Tabernacle in New York City for almost forty years. By the time he died in 1937, he had authored more than a dozen books—including *The Minister As Shepherd*, the volume I had spent months trying to locate. The talks that constitute this delightful book were originally delivered at Bangor Theological Seminary for the George Shepard Lectures on Preaching. In my opinion, Wiersbe judged their value expertly.

What a profound book this is! And yet, how simple. Time after time Pastor Jefferson goes to the heart of the matter and lays out with piercing biblical vision the place, the role, and the necessity of the pastor as shepherd. For example, Jefferson discusses with great insight why the shepherd metaphor carries such power:

> One of the secrets of the fascination of "shepherd" as a title is that the word carries us straight to Christ himself. It associates us at once with him. So far as the New Testament tells us, Jesus never called himself a priest, or

a preacher, or a rector, or a clergyman, or a bishop, or an elder, but he liked to think of himself as a shepherd. The shepherd idea was often in his mind.... Jesus had many metaphors by which to image forth his character and his office, but the metaphor by which he loved best to paint his portrait was shepherd.[1]

And what kind of proof would Pastor Jefferson offer in support of this observation?

Peter was a fisherman, and could have best understood, presumably, the language native to a fisherman's lips, but Jesus in his final charge to the son of Jonas used only the vocabulary of the sheepfold. "Feed my lambs. Tend my sheep. Feed my sheep." In other words: "Be a shepherd, and do a shepherd's work." The great shepherd of the sheep in framing a charge which he deemed sufficient for the guidance and encouragement of the leaders of the Christian church down to the end of time, used only a shepherd's speech. The history of the church begins with Jesus saying to the leader who is to head the work of discipling the nations: "I am a shepherd, be thou a shepherd too."[2]

Pastor Jefferson then informed his listeners (and readers) that the early church both heard and recognized its Master's emphasis on the shepherd. That is why the figure of a shepherd can be found on thousands of early Christian tombs, on chalices used for the Lord's Supper, in churches and chapels, on lamps, on rings, and on countless sarcophagi. In fact, he concludes, the shepherd "was the first favorite symbol of Christian life and faith."[3]

Yet somehow, somewhere along the way, the church largely abandoned this God-given metaphor as the working blueprint for its pastors. The result? Discouragement, decline, and ultimately disaster. In Jefferson's words:

When church leaders began to lose the vision of the good shepherd, they at the same time began to drift away from the New Testament ideal of ministerial service. Little by little they magnified their office in ways not sanctioned by the good shepherd of the sheep. . . . The church lost the way which leads to life as soon as the envoys of the Son of God forgot that they were shepherds.[4]

WHEN FORGETFULNESS BECOMES FATAL

Loss of memory always devastates, and the more momentous the memory loss, the more devastating the consequences. To Pastor Jefferson, no greater disaster could have befallen the church than that its "envoys" (you and me) forgot they were meant to be shepherds.

I think he's right. I can't help but wonder if this forgetfulness lies at the heart of most of our church troubles. Our general lack of impact, our ineffectiveness, our dismissal by the culture at large, our stagnant growth, our high rates of pastoral burnout, our low degree of parishioner involvement—what are these but symptoms that the church has "lost the way which leads to life"?

Way back in 1912, Pastor Jefferson offered his diagnosis of the problem: Pastors had forgotten that they were called, first of all, to be shepherds of the sheep. Nearly a century has passed since the publication of *The Minister As Shepherd*, but still the patient lies in the infirmary. Did Jefferson misdiagnose the problem? No. But the patient has demanded second opinions, third opinions, fourth opinions—"The problem is, pastors don't know how to manage." "No, the real problem is that churches need good bus programs." "No, the problem is that pastors don't know how to lead"—and has never sought treatment for the original, correct diagnosis. The root system is diseased, and so the symptoms of disease continue to spread, multiply, and intensify.

As much as I admire Jefferson's ability to identify the cause of our ecclesiastical ills, I must point out, however, that he was far from the first to do so. In fact, thousands of years before the publication of his insightful book, other "spiritual doctors" had already made the same diagnosis. What happens when God's leaders fail to take seriously the shepherd's role? The Old Testament prophets Jeremiah and Ezekiel saw firsthand what happens, and we can gain much insight from their difficult experiences as well as from their ancient prescriptions!

A BAD TIME IN THE OLD TOWN TONIGHT

Jeremiah and Ezekiel lived in dark, sad times. Jeremiah, the older of the two prophets, lived and prophesied during the reigns of five of Judah's kings, from Josiah to Zedekiah. His ministry began around 626 B.C. and ended sometime after 586. He predicted (and lived to see) the destruction of Jerusalem and its temple as a result of the faithlessness of its people. He was there in 605 B.C. when the Babylonian king, Nebuchadnezzar, attacked Jerusalem for the first time and carried off Daniel and some of Judah's best young minds. Jeremiah was there in 597 B.C. when King Jehoiakim, Ezekiel, and another large group of Jewish captives were taken by force to Babylon, and he was still ministering when Nebuchadnezzar sacked Jerusalem, broke down its walls, and burned both its buildings and its temple to the ground. Jeremiah saw sad days, indeed.

Anyone familiar with the Bible knows that these calamities struck Judah, and Israel before her, because the Lord's people had turned away from the living God to idols. Centuries earlier, God had warned his people through Moses that he would respond to Israelite rebellion and unfaithfulness by scattering his people to the four winds:

> If you do not carefully follow all the words of this law
> ... then the LORD will scatter you among all nations, from
> one end of the earth to the other. . . . Among those nations
> you will find no repose, no resting place for the sole of

your foot. There the LORD will give you an anxious mind, eyes weary with longing, and a despairing heart. You will live in constant suspense, filled with dread both night and day, never sure of your life. (Deuteronomy 28:58, 64–66)

Before we resurrect the diagnoses of Drs. Jeremiah and Ezekiel regarding their failing patient Judah, I cannot help but notice that many of the symptoms listed in this passage ("an anxious mind, eyes weary with longing, and a despairing heart") mark thousands of our contemporary churches. Could it be that the virus that infected ancient Judah and Israel has returned today in a mutated form?

I think the answer is probably "yes." But to be sure, let us consult these two ancient physicians of the Israelite soul. Perhaps their findings can offer us both instruction and hope.

IN SEARCH OF SHEPHERDS WITH JEREMIAH

Scholars tell us that one of the primary titles to be applied to any ruler in the ancient Near East was "shepherd." For example, the *Theological Wordbook of the Old Testament* declares:

> From very ancient antiquity, rulers were described as demonstrating their legitimacy to rule by their ability to "pasture" their people. Hammurabi and many other rulers of ancient western Asia are called "shepherd" or described as "pasturing" their subjects.[5]

This is important to keep in mind when we read about "shepherds" in Jeremiah and Ezekiel, because the prophets do not have in view priests or Levites. When they speak of Judah's shepherds, they are referring to its officers and leaders, whether spiritual or governmental. Of course, in ancient times the line between leaders of government and leaders of religion was not drawn as sharply as it is today; kings were expected to lead the way in spiritual matters, just as prophets and priests were expected to influence public policy. The critical point to remember is that leaders in biblical times were seen, first and foremost, as shepherds of the flock entrusted to their care.

In this context, consider the first diagnosis Jeremiah delivers regarding his patient, the ailing Judah. He does not point to poor techniques or deficient strategies as the cause of his patient's ill health, but to Judah's erring shepherds. "The shepherds are senseless and do not inquire of the LORD," he declares, "so they do not prosper and all their flock is scattered" (Jeremiah 10:21).

The term translated "senseless" comes from the Hebrew *ba<ar*, "a brutish person." Its root "seems to contrast man's ability to reason and understand with the beast's inability to do so."[6] The standard Hebrew lexicon says this word refers to a person who is "*dull-hearted*, ignorant of God.'"[7]

Why were these shepherds senseless? Why were they called brutish, beastly, dull-hearted, and ignorant of God? Jeremiah answers, because they did not "inquire of the LORD." So we gain our initial insight: Failure to inquire of the Lord *always* results in brutish, beastly, dull-hearted ignorance of God that inevitably leads to disaster.

What does this mean for us? I think it means that if we are serious about nursing the church back to robust health, we must first recognize our utter need for the Lord. Stiff-necked self-sufficiency and the continual pursuit of other alternatives marked these ancient leaders . . . and many of today's. We need to continually confess the preeminence of God himself. Recognition of our sin and repentance always precede any remedy provided by God. Only then can we ask the Lord for his guidance to find the proper course of action.

So, what does God tell us? He informs us that we have missed the opening page of our diagnostic textbooks. We have forgotten that he has called us to be, first and foremost, shepherds of the sheep.

How can we expect to make a correct diagnosis if we have skipped the very first step in our spiritual training? No wonder our flocks do not prosper; no wonder the sheep seem scattered. The church may produce an abundance of leaders and managers and pulpiteers and CEOs and vision-casters, but it will continue to falter if it does not have at the helm shepherds who long to "inquire of the LORD."

"Do you want to avoid the disaster that befell Judah?" Jeremiah might ask us today. "Do you want to find your way back to health, back to prosperity and influence and true success? Then start at the beginning: Find shepherds who love to inquire of the Lord. That is the beginning. That is the way to recovery. That is the only way."

Two chapters after this first consultation, Jeremiah continues to probe and peer into the root causes of the disease laying waste to his people. In 12:10–11 the prophet writes:

> Many shepherds will ruin my vineyard
>   and trample down my field;
> they will turn my pleasant field
>   into a desolate wasteland.
> It will be made a wasteland,
>   parched and desolate before me;
> the whole land will be laid waste
>   because there is no one who cares.

I take this declaration to be the prophet's central diagnosis, his identification of the root cause of Judah's apostasy. Once again, the shepherds take center stage. Jeremiah says that they "ruin my [God's] vineyard" and "trample down my field." They turn the green pasture into a "desolate wasteland," "parched" and "laid waste." What a terrible scene!

But how did it get that way? What caused this desolation, this awful devastation? What did the shepherds do to bring about such a catastrophe? Simple, explains Jeremiah. They just didn't care.

They didn't care? That's it? What about greed? What about lust for power? What about the desire for comfort? What about the hankering for prestige, for acclaim, for influence or riches or special favors? What about any of those things or a thousand like them?

No, says Jeremiah. None of those things came first. The core problem with Judah's shepherds is that they simply did not care about their sheep. In other respects they may have been good leaders, great managers, super facilitators. Yet none of that mattered in the end. What mattered is that *they didn't care* ... and Judah died.

Still, Jeremiah is not yet finished. In his longest passage on the fatal shortcomings of Judah's shepherds, he utters this frightful condemnation:

> "Woe to the shepherds who are destroying and scattering the sheep of my pasture!" declares the LORD. Therefore this is what the LORD, the God of Israel, says to the shepherds who tend my people: "Because you have scattered my flock and driven them away and have not bestowed care on them, I will bestow punishment on you for the evil you have done," declares the LORD. (Jeremiah 23:1–2)

It should sober us to realize how often God begins an address to spiritual leaders with the dreadful word "woe." It is one of those unmistakable words that instantly conveys the idea, "You're walking on an icy, sloping path covered with banana peels, a scant six inches from a bottomless pit, and a six-ton boulder is hurtling toward you." It is not an encouraging word.

Yet that is how God addressed the shepherds of Judah in Jeremiah's day. Condemned because they had destroyed, scattered, and driven away the sheep of God's pasture, the Lord proclaimed judgment on them: "Because you have ... not bestowed care on them, I will bestow punishment on you" (Jeremiah 23:2).

The literary focal point of this passage is the Hebrew word *paqad*, a term that can express both positive ("bestow care") and negative ("bestow punishment") ideas. One authority explains, "The basic meaning [of this word] is to exercise oversight over a subordinate, either in the form of inspecting or of taking action to cause a considerable change in the circumstances of the subordinate, either for the better or for the worse."[8] Jeremiah uses the word in both its positive and negative senses in this verse. The prophet employs a frightful wordplay to announce to the foolish shepherds that because they did not "bestow care on" (*paqad*) the sheep, God would "bestow punishment on" (*paqad*) them.

Once again, God makes it clear that shepherds in his service are given one overriding duty that supersedes all others: to "bestow care on" his sheep. Not to manage them (although that must be done). Not to inspire them (although that, too, is necessary). Not even to lead them (as indispensable as that is). No. The primary concern of a shepherd in the service of the Lord should be to "bestow care on" his sheep—and if a shepherd fails in this most fundamental of duties, God promises to "bestow punishment" on the shepherd.

WHAT WAS TRUE THEN IS ALSO TRUE TODAY

"But wait!" someone may object. "That was true in the Old Testament under the old covenant, but times have changed. By God's grace, we no longer live under the law. What Jeremiah said of Israel's ancient shepherds no longer applies."

Doesn't it? I wonder. The book of Jude appears to confirm, rather than overturn, the threatening scenario laid out by Jeremiah. Jude wrote to a New Testament church that had been infiltrated by "shepherds" who were "blemishes at your love feasts, eating with you without the slightest qualm—shepherds who feed only themselves" (Jude 12). Sounds a lot like the shepherds of Jeremiah's day, doesn't it? So what is Jude's word for them? "They are wild waves of the sea, foaming up their shame; wandering stars, for whom blackest darkness has been reserved forever" (v. 13). In other words, even new covenant shepherds who fail to "bestow care on" the sheep can expect that God will "bestow punishment on" them.

Let me say it plainly. I believe God's rebuke and discipline lie on many today who call themselves pastors. Why? Because although they may be fine vision-casters, although they may be great managers, although they may exhibit strong leadership qualities, they do not particularly care for their sheep. In all honesty, I live with a healthy fear of that. I do not want God's judgment to fall on me. Yet I believe that if I am not living out the role to which God has called me, I will receive his judgment and discipline. I remember—and shudder—that God took everything away from the Old Testament shepherds, and I don't want anything like that to come near me.

Consider this. God did not chastise Judah's shepherds for leading the people astray but for failing to care for their sheep. The flock scattered and wandered away from God because the shepherds didn't care, not because they didn't lead. Bad leadership *resulted* from their lack of concern. Because they didn't *care*, they led the sheep astray. Certainly shepherds must lead their flocks, but that is emphatically *not* their first duty. It intrigues me that God's rebuke comes because of the relational aspects of the shepherd's role, not on its technical aspects. Judah's leaders weren't wolves, just bad shepherds. They remind us that, first and foremost, the shepherd is one who cares for the sheep.

Two other passages in Jeremiah put an exclamation point on God's judgment against these uncaring shepherds. In Jeremiah 25:34–36, the Lord declares:

Weep and wail, you shepherds;
    roll in the dust, you leaders of the flock.
For your time to be slaughtered has come;
    you will fall and be shattered like fine pottery.
The shepherds will have nowhere to flee,
    the leaders of the flock no place to escape.
Hear the cry of the shepherds,
    the wailing of the leaders of the flock,
    for the LORD is destroying their pasture.

This prophetic word began to be fulfilled in 597 B.C. when Nebuchadnezzar laid siege to Jerusalem and took captive King Jehoiachin, his mother, his attendants, his nobles and officials, as well as all the officers, fighting men, craftsmen, and artisans—a total of ten thousand prisoners (2 Kings 24:12–16). God's word against Judah's shepherds was no hollow threat.

Jeremiah's final word concerning his nation's shepherds appears in Jeremiah 50:6, where the prophet writes:

My people have been lost sheep;
    their shepherds have led them astray
    and caused them to roam on the mountains.
They wandered over mountain and hill
    and forgot their own resting place.

The word translated "led astray" here is the Hebrew term *ta<ah*, which means "to err" or "to cause to wander about."[9] The most familiar biblical passage in which this term is employed is Isaiah 53:6, "where the physical and spiritual nuances blend beautifully: 'All we like sheep have gone astray. . . .'"[10]

So yes, these ancient shepherds led their people astray. But why? Because they did not care for them. They did not love their sheep, their leadership reflected this lack of love, and, as a result, the people "wandered over mountain and hill and forgot their own resting place."

IN SEARCH OF SHEPHERDS WITH EZEKIEL

The sorry story gets no better when we turn to Ezekiel, the prophet carried into exile by the Babylonians in 597 B.C. In 34:1–10, Ezekiel reports:

> The word of the LORD came to me: "Son of man, prophesy against the shepherds of Israel; prophesy and say to them: 'This is what the Sovereign LORD says: Woe to the shepherds of Israel who only take care of themselves! Should not shepherds take care of the flock? You eat the curds, clothe yourselves with the wool and slaughter the choice animals, but you do not take care of the flock. You have not strengthened the weak or healed the sick or bound up the injured. You have not brought back the strays or searched for the lost. You have ruled them harshly and brutally. So they were scattered because there was no shepherd, and when they were scattered they became food for all the wild animals. My sheep wandered over all the mountains and on every high hill. They were scattered over the whole earth, and no one searched or looked for them.
>
> "'Therefore, you shepherds, hear the word of the LORD: As surely as I live, declares the Sovereign LORD, because my flock lacks a shepherd and so has been plundered and has become food for all the wild animals, and because my shepherds did not search for my flock but cared for themselves rather than for my flock, therefore, O shepherds, hear the word of the LORD: This is what the Sovereign LORD says: I am against the shepherds and will hold them accountable for my flock. I will remove them from tending the flock so that the shepherds can no longer feed themselves. I will rescue my flock from their mouths, and it will no longer be food for them.'"

While Ezekiel's complaint against the shepherds of Israel virtually mirrors the charges of his elder colleague, the younger prophet does spell out in more detail both what the shepherds had done wrong and what they had left undone. Consider his laundry list of offenses:

What They Did	*What They Left Undone*
Took care only of themselves Ate curds Clothed themselves with wool Slaughtered the choice sheep Ruled the sheep harshly and brutally	Did not strengthen the weak Did not heal the sick Did not bind up the injured Did not bring back strays Did not search for the lost

Ezekiel tells us that when shepherds commit the offenses listed above, the result is threefold: (1) The sheep are scattered; (2) the sheep become food for wild animals; and (3) the sheep wander on every high hill. In contemporary terms, when God's people are led by pastors who lack a shepherd's heart, at least three things tend to happen: (1) People splinter into cliques and never develop the kind of congregational fellowship designed by God; (2) they become much more susceptible to the blandishments both of cultic groups and of charlatans out to plunder them; and (3) they tend to leave behind sound doctrine and a vibrant relationship with God in search of more and more aberrant teachings that promise some kind of spiritual "buzz."

Finally, one more thing happens: God removes these shepherds from their posts.

All these offenses can be summed up in the first complaint Ezekiel lists against the wicked shepherds: They refused to take care of the flock and instead took care only of themselves. When the Hebrew term *ra<ah*, here translated "take care of," appears as a noun, it is normally translated "shepherd." The term is "the primary term for 'feeding' domestic animals. Since the most common occupation in Palestine from greatest antiquity was shepherding, the term is basic to the description of the people of the country in all historical periods."[11] That is why the

> failure of the officers of Israel to feed the people either physical or spiritual nourishment was deemed a severe transgression (Ezk 24:2ff.). In this chapter the prophet plays repeatedly on the two forms of the root, . . . the verb meaning "to pasture" and the noun meaning the "pastor" or shepherd. The true repetition of the ideas is lost in all the versions by supplying synonyms where the Hebrew uses the same term throughout.[12]

Ralph Alexander, in his commentary on Ezekiel, writes of these leaders,

> They had failed to provide for the needy—those weak and sick. They had not sought for sheep that had been lost. They did not care what happened to the people as long as they as leaders had all their own personal needs met. They were harsh and brutal in their rule (v. 4). God makes it clear that a leader has a primary responsibility to care for those he leads, even at the sacrifice of his own desires. Would that political and spiritual leaders both then and now would recognize this heart attitude of leadership![13]

Amen! We must come to see that the primary duty of those whom God calls to lead his church is *caring for the sheep*—not managing, not directing, not vision-casting, not anything else. Shepherds who fail to care for their sheep—that is, leaders who neglect to strengthen the weak, heal the sick, bind up the injured, bring back the strays, or search for the lost—are in danger of losing their privileged position and of incurring the discipline of God.

Just in case we forget the critical importance God attaches to this shepherdly role, let me end this section by quoting a third prophet, Zechariah, a priest born in Babylonia who returned to Judah in 538 B.C. with Zerubbabel, a descendant of David, and others to rebuild the Jerusalem temple. As if to remind the Israelites, who at last were returning to their homeland from captivity in a pagan land, that their problems all stemmed from bad leadership, the Lord declares through Zechariah, "My anger burns against the shepherds, and I will punish the leaders; for the LORD Almighty will care for his flock, the house of Judah, and make them like a proud horse in battle" (Zechariah 10:3).

I think we could use a few proud horses in battle, don't you?

LET'S GET BACK TO THE BASICS!

For too long we have neglected the leadership model that God has both authorized and illustrated. Repeatedly God referred to the leaders of Israel as shepherds. I have heard it said that we can glean leadership principles by studying the errors of Israel's shepherds. However, when you look at the text carefully, you see that God did not rebuke these men for leading the flock astray but for failing to care. Their sin was not poor leadership but poor shepherdship. Because these shepherds did not care, their sheep wandered away.

Problem: The heart of a shepherd never beat in these leaders' chests.

Result: The people were led astray and turned away from God.

It wasn't that these leaders lacked a vision for the future or that they failed to inspire confidence. It was not that they abandoned good management principles or disregarded sound leadership theory or even that they neglected to hear what their constituents were telling them. The kindling that fueled the conflagration to come was that *they didn't care for the sheep.* That, God says, is what lit the match that burned down the ancient Jewish nation.

That is one reason why not even the term favored by many today to refer to pastors, *servant-leaders*, hits the bull's-eye. The problem of these ancient shepherds wasn't so much that they failed to *serve* as that they failed to *care*. One can serve without caring, which is why the apostle Paul warns us in 1 Corinthians 13:3 that it is possible to "give all I possess to the poor and surrender my body to the flames"—certainly remarkable examples of service!—and yet in the end "gain nothing." How is that possible? Because one can do all that and still "have not love." In other words, it isn't *service* that guards leaders against ineffectiveness and abuse of power, but *love*; not *technique*, but *concern*; not *keen insight*, but *genuine caring*—which is exactly the characteristic at the top of a shepherd's job description!

So, then, all of us called into the pastorate must ask ourselves: Do we care for the sheep?

Now, that does not mean we don't get angry at the sheep once in awhile. We all get frustrated or irritated with them, but even that comes because we care. Even in this we follow the pattern given to us by our Lord.

The heart of God is grieved at what his sheep sometimes do and don't do. How often in the Scriptures do we see that the Great Shepherd grieves over his sheep? In a similar way, our hearts will be grieved as well. Paul wrote to one particularly difficult church:

> I am afraid that when I come I may not find you as I want you to be. . . . I fear that there may be quarreling, jealousy, outbursts of anger, factions, slander, gossip, arrogance and disorder. I am afraid that when I come again my God will humble me before you, and I will be grieved over many who have sinned earlier and have not repented of the impurity, sexual sin and debauchery in which they have indulged. (2 Corinthians 12:20–21)

A shepherd's job includes pain, hardship, and even heartache. "Who is weak, and I do not feel weak?" the apostle asked. "Who is led into sin, and I do not inwardly burn?" (2 Corinthians 11:29).

Even beyond this, we must realize that some sheep simply don't want to be led. But why should we be surprised? If New Testament sheep spurned and attacked even such a seasoned shepherd as the apostle Paul—remember, he devotes extended portions of his Galatian and Corinthian letters to a defense of his ministry—then who are we to think that our own sheep will never turn on us? Yet even if they turn on us, still we must care!

Pastor and author David Fisher described a time when some anonymous sheep in his flock decided that he needed to go—despite the church board's unanimous support of his ministry and the affirmation of the congregation as a whole. "It devastated me," he wrote. "I felt horrible. The pastoral instinct to care deeply came home to haunt me. It usually does. The more we care, the more rejection hurts. That's the way it is with love."[14]

I remind my staff all the time that once we view certain sheep in an adversarial way, our ministry is over. That's the uniqueness of the Chief Shepherd. He loved even Judas, whom he knew would eventually betray him. That is a mark of a true shepherd.

I love the ministry, but I would be less than truthful if I claimed that all of it has been smooth sailing. I remember one time when not one, but three people to whom we were close, died in the space of less than two weeks. I had just been with one family for more than twelve hours, watching a dear friend die and ministering to his kids and grandkids as they approached his deathbed to say their last good-byes. Hour after hour, I talked with the doctors and helped this child or that grandchild get closure with Dad and Granddad. I arrived home that day at 3:00 A.M., sat on the edge of the bed with my head in my hands, and wept over my sheep and the pain in their lives. "It's too hard," I told Susan. "It hurts too much. I don't know if I can do it anymore."

"If it didn't hurt," my dear wife replied wisely, "you wouldn't be an effective pastor." Pain is a part of caring, and caring for the sheep is a part of shepherding.

It struck me later that, somewhere along the line, God would mature me as a shepherd to be able to hold on to some of these emotions so that I am not dominated by them, but without losing this dimension of deep caring. I never want to become so callused that I can say, "Well, I just lost one more person from the bottom line. I wonder how it's going to affect the offerings next week?"

Yesterday I was talking on the phone with a pastor friend who lives out west. He was describing his economic stresses and detailing how much he was traveling, speaking, and writing each month to earn extra money to pay his kids' college tuition. We asked each other, "How long can we do this?" He cares deeply for his people; he weeps with them often and prays with them. "It would be a whole lot easier, wouldn't it," he suggested, "if we just went to the corner office and ran things? Wrote our magnificent sermons. I don't know if I've got another fifteen or twenty years of being a pastor. I don't know if I can take it, emotionally and physiologically."

It is so easy to shift into a caretaker mode or to take on the CEO role. I could easily do that for another twenty years; that would be no big deal. It is easy to run a church and to stay out of people's lives. In fact, we have a phrase for pastors who stay in their churches but check out of ministry. I'll ask, "How is pastor so-and-so doing?" And I'll hear, "Oh, he's retired." He's still a full-time pastor, but he's retired. The pain and grief just weren't worth it any longer, so he checked out. As I told my friend, "It would be much easier if we didn't hang out with the sheep—but both of us would be repulsed by that."

Still, we both struggle with the demands of trying to be true shepherds. My friend has done everything he can to make ends meet, as has his church. He is knocking himself out because he doesn't want to leave his sheep. Things got complicated a while back when a ministry offered him a job for significantly more money than he is currently making. While my friend doesn't completely agree with that group's theology, that didn't make his decision any easier. He told me, "You know, if I weren't a pastor, I'd take it. But that's not my calling." His whole frame of reference is that he is called to the particular flock of sheep he now pastors. For him it's not an economic decision; it's not a career advancement decision. It's a decision of calling, of faithfulness to God's will for his life.

When I first announced that I was leaving Promise Keepers to pastor Calvary Church, some well-meaning but misguided people told me, "Glenn, this is really going to advance your career." They made the comment because Calvary has a long and rich history and is positioned to make a significant impact for the kingdom. But their statement betrays an executive mind-set that dominates the thinking of today's American church—Corporate Christianity.

To be honest, I was offended by their comments. After all, if I wanted to sell books, appear on the radio or television, and be invited to speak at major conferences and events, what could be better than to remain on the leadership team of a prominent, nationwide parachurch ministry? That is not why I left.

God has called me to be a pastor, and the Lord called me to shepherd these particular sheep. I walked *away* from notoriety; I didn't step *into* it. I am not looking for television or radio fame. I want to shepherd God's flock. That's the whole reason for this book. I also believe it is the key to creating an effective church—but until we get there, success will continue to elude us.

TRUE, BUT NOT NEW

None of the insights in this chapter were new to Charles Edward Jefferson, the pastor we met earlier, who back in 1912 championed the idea that pastors ought to be, first and foremost, shepherds of God's sheep. He knew as well as anyone that many of those who desire to hold leadership positions in the local church have no desire to shepherd. That is why he wrote, "The work of the shepherd was an abomination, we are told, to the ancient Egyptians, and so it is to all pulpit Pharaohs who are interested in building pyramids out of eloquent words."[15]

Jefferson also knew that shepherding is hard, arduous work and that it often involves pain of a type that makes many would-be pastors shudder.

> It is by no means easy for a young man to become a shepherd, and he ought not to be discouraged if he cannot become one in a day, or a year. An orator he can be without difficulty. A reformer he can become at once. In criticism of politics and society he can do a flourishing business the first Sunday. But a shepherd he can become only slowly, and by patiently traveling the way of the cross.
>
> The shepherd's work is a humble work; such it has been from the beginning and such it must be to the end. A man must come down to it. A shepherd cannot shine. He cannot cut a figure. His work must be done in obscurity.... It is a form of service which eats up a man's life. It makes a man old before his time. Every good shepherd lays down his life for the sheep.[16]

But Jefferson also knew at least two other secrets that many of us have forgotten. First, people are crying out for true shepherds whose hearts overflow with loving care for the sheep. He explains, "The heart of a man is like the heart of a sheep, it beats at the sight of a shepherd."[17] Second, Jefferson knew that people long for caring shepherds because they are created with exactly that thirst.

A few things are certain. We live in a universe created by a Shepherd God. The Lord is our Shepherd. Our world is redeemed by a Shepherd Saviour. Our elder brother is a shepherd. The man whom humanity most needs is a shepherd. Every messenger of Christ is sent to do a shepherd's work. We are to stand at last before a shepherd Judge. God is going to separate the good shepherds from the shepherds who are bad. The questions which every pastor must meet and answer are three: "Did you feed my lambs? Did you tend my sheep? Did you feed my sheep?"[18]

In our love affair with all models contemporary, we have left behind the model that God himself both authorized and illustrated. The one model, the one role, that the Lord highlights for us in both Old and New Testament is that of shepherd.

As hard as Jeremiah could be on the shepherds of his day, he also looked ahead to a happier time when God promised: "I will give you shepherds after my own heart, who will lead you with knowledge and understanding" (Jeremiah 3:15).

Could it be that you are one such pastor? Is it possible that your own pastor would gladly become such a shepherd, if only he received some warm encouragement from his sheep? I hope so, because therein lies the hope of the church.

Chapter 3

....

A DISASTROUS SHIFT

....

A thick tension hung in the air. On one side stood an angry group of scholars, determined to expose the serious errors and dangerous viewpoints of a brash peasant who held crowds spellbound with his insightful rhetoric. On the other side stood the offending young man and his enthusiastic fans. Bystanders wondered who would win the debate this time (it wasn't the first clash). Much to the displeasure of the scholars, it seemed that the audience was pulling for the brash, young peasant.

When the scholars' chance came, they seized it with a snarling, smug confidence. In front of everyone, they demanded that the young peasant answer a thorny question—a question obviously designed to embarrass and perplex him—and everyone in the crowd held their breath waiting to hear how their favorite might answer. No one was prepared for the sharpness of his reply.

"You are in error," began Jesus, "because you do not know the Scriptures or the power of God" (Matthew 22:29).

ERROR FOLLOWS IGNORANCE

Error never trails far behind ignorance of God's Word and disregard for his power. Whenever we fail to take into account the Lord's divine wisdom and his infinite ability to do whatever he pleases, we fall into error—serious error.

In the case described above, the error occurred when the Sadducees elevated human reasoning and earthly philosophy over the teaching of the Bible. They compounded their error when they dismissed heaven's power to fulfill its promises. When Jesus said they didn't "know" the Scriptures, he didn't mean they were unacquainted with them. In fact, the Sadducees introduced their loaded question by saying, "Moses told us that . . . ," a clear indication that they *were* familiar with the Torah. They knew it, but they didn't *know* it. They could recite it, but they didn't believe it. They could quote it, but they didn't live by it.

You know, this sounds eerily familiar to me. I wonder if the spirit of the Sadducees isn't alive and thriving among us even today. Our problem in today's church runs deeper than a mere infatuation with the latest technique or craze. For the past few decades we have increasingly turned away from biblical and theological models and clamored after sociological and psychological ones. While we continue to insist that the Bible is our final rule of faith and practice, in reality we rely on more "practical" tools fashioned in the worlds of business or academia.

In particular, we have discarded biblical theology in favor of what we have come to call "practical ministry." The church is now driven by sociological and psychological phenomena rather than by biblical imperatives and scriptural guidelines—and it's been that way for some time.

Back in 1954, H. R. Niebuhr called the pastorate "the perplexed profession" because pastors no longer knew who they were. What had so confused them? The cause was not hard to identify. As Seward Hiltner wrote several years later, "The pastoral ministry has no unifying theory by which it organizes itself. The ministry is no longer based on a theology."

Then what *was* it based on? David Fisher, author of *The 21st Century Pastor*, insists that even today "there is no accepted theology of the ministry. . . . Instead, the practice of ministry has become the theology. The task itself is the model."[1] In other words, we have abandoned God's idea of the ministry in order to pursue our own vision of how ministry ought to be done. And because we have chosen not to "know the Scriptures or the power of God," we have fallen into error . . . and inevitable decline. We're the Sadducees, Part II.

PLAYING THE SEMINARY SHIFT

So how did we get into this mess we've created for ourselves? We can trace much of the trouble to our seminaries at the turn of the century, when courses in *pastoral* theology began to be dropped in favor of new offerings in *practical* theology. The schools believed they were sending their students out into the churches without sufficient instruction in the "nuts and bolts" of ministry—how to conduct weddings, funerals, counseling, and the like—so they began to change their curricula to focus more on the practical aspects of ministry.

Unfortunately, they went too far. In fact, these days it is difficult to find a seminary track in pastoral theology that is solidly rooted in the Scriptures. Most seminaries now teach "practical ministry," a set of learned skills rooted in psychological and sociological principles. This approach isn't theological in the true sense of the term, for practical ministry is a *philosophical* and *programmatic* approach to conducting ministry. With few exceptions, courses teaching "pastoral theology" have been replaced by newer offerings in "practical ministry." All this implies ever so subtly that what the Bible has to say about pastoral ministry may be helpful in a limited ideological sense but that anyone who wants a ministry that truly works must discover the *real* nuts and bolts elsewhere.

If you don't believe me, pick up a recent issue of *Leadership* or *Christianity Today* and look at the ads for the various seminaries. The one thing you probably *won't* see is a biblically focused pitch for the training and equipping of those who want to be pastors.

So if seminarians aren't reading pastoral theology, what are they studying? More than likely they are receiving a heavy dose of resources such as *The One Minute Manager* and instruction from "leadership experts" such as Peter Drucker. Today's seminary graduate could very well write a philosophy of ministry quoting DuPree and Drucker but neither Baxter nor the Bible. It used to be said that theology was the queen of the sciences, but no more. For the most part, theology isn't even the queen of the *seminaries*.

I want to be careful here. I do not oppose what Drucker or others are saying. In fact, I have read all their books and benefited greatly from them. My concern, rather, is that when merely human ideas (no matter how good they might be) are substituted for sound theology, we have no way to ensure that these ideas will be used in a way that conforms to and honors Scripture.

To make matters worse, the absence of sound theological training leaves seminarians ill-equipped to minister God's Word and shepherd God's flock in the real world. If you were to ask most seminarians today to describe a biblical philosophy of ministry, they probably wouldn't have much to say. That's what happens in the absence of a sound theological foundation.

Of course, I don't think we do anything apart from our theological presuppositions, whether they are right or wrong, examined or unexamined. So why do we think we can ask people who lack a proper theological foundation to tend and care for eternal souls? How can they rightly operate on those souls? Yet we continue to put young men and women in the front lines of spiritual warfare with no biblical arsenal to sustain them. Isn't there something in the Bible about putting on the whole armor of God?

For some reason we have developed in our seminaries a ministry model based on psychological and sociological data rather than on the core of Scripture. I tend to agree with speaker and author Os Guinness, who has argued that the heresy of the twentieth-century church was turning helpful mechanisms into destructive ones by failing to deploy them on a proper foundation. To use a football analogy, we have tried to run the West Coast Offense with junior-high kids on the line. It just doesn't work.

PUBLISHING JOINS THE SHIFT

This shift from theology to pragmatism can be seen just as clearly in the publishing world as in the halls of academia. It intrigues me that no more than a handful of books written in the last few years focus directly on the issue of pastoral theology. Thomas Oden, professor of theology at Drew University, published his own *Pastoral Theology* in 1983 and lamented in the preface that "regrettably, the deliberate study of the pastoral office and its functions (traditionally called pastoral theology) has been neglected in our time."[2] Later he added:

> Pastoral theology as a unifying discipline was flourishing a century ago and remained robust until the beginning of this century, yet it has largely faded into such hazy memory that none of its best representatives is still in print. We hope to hammer out a rudimentary pastoral theology half as good as any of a dozen that were available a century ago.[3]

It is no wonder, then, that Oden's extensive bibliography (a full thirty-four pages!) lists almost nothing from recent years; nearly every work dates from the nineteenth century or before. No one seems to be turning out classic

texts dealing with pastoral theology. The discipline has simply disappeared off our theological radar screens.

To find really good material on pastoral theology, or
poimenics, as it was termed in earlier times, one must look
to centuries past. "The eighteenth and nineteenth centuries
spoke of 'poimenics,'" explains Seward Hiltner. "This
meant the study of shepherding since it came from the
Greek word for shepherd, *poimen*, which in turn came from
a verb form that meant to feed or to tend the flock."[4]

Who writes of *poimenics* or "shepherdology" today? Not
many. Why not? Because virtually everything written these
days issues from secular management and leadership theory. As David Fisher has noted:

> Somewhere along the way the old theological disci-
> pline called "pastoral theology" was lost. For centuries
> each theological tradition had a classic pastoral theology
> text, and pastoral theology was a central part of the theo-
> logical curriculum. Around the turn of the century, pas-
> toral theology disappeared, and in conservative quarters
> it was replaced by "practical theology"—"how-to" pas-
> toral training. In the mainline churches "pastoral care," in
> which the pastor became primarily a counselor, was the
> new discipline. In most of American Protestantism, bibli-
> cal and theological reflection on pastoral ministry ceased.
> The practice of ministry became the theology of ministry.
>
> Hiltner's *Preface to Pastoral Theology* changed the face
> of pastoral ministry in America. Protesting the lack of a
> pastoral theology, Hiltner proposed a psychological/soci-
> ological base as a unifying theory for ministry. "Pastoral
> care" became increasingly therapeutic. "Shepherding,"
> the ancient practice of the cure of souls, became more and
> more counseling. Clinical pastoral education moved to
> the center of pastoral training.
>
> Because the base was social science, not theology, the
> pastoral art was reduced to human skill. The transcen-
> dent dimension of ministry, its grounding in God himself,

was removed from pastoral theology. In fact, theology itself disappeared as the practical work of ministry was removed from seminary theology departments to a practical vision that tended to describe pastoral ministry in human terms. Biblical and theological reflection on pastoral ministry soon faded away. Reflection on the church and its ministry was separated from the body of theology and is now conducted on a largely human level.[5]

Like a satellite passing silently overhead, the magnitude of this truth escapes us, yet it was a shift both radical and disastrous. Pastoral theology moved from being a crucial part of the canon of church literature to nothing more than a distant memory!

More than two decades ago, Jay Adams noted that, while evangelicals continued to steadfastly ignore pastoral theology, their liberal and neo-orthodox counterparts were beginning once more to pay attention to this dusty old discipline. Adams could not let this unsettling observation pass without comment ... and a warning.

> There has been a revival of interest in the theology of pastoral activity, particularly among liberal and neo-orthodox writers. While the interest must be welcomed, one cannot refrain from observing that the conclusions reached by beginning with unscriptural views of God and man have been universally unsatisfactory. On the other hand, many conservative writers have all but failed to recognize the implications of theology in writing about pastoral care. Often unwittingly, they have applied themselves to the task with fuzzy or erroneous theological thinking that ends in similarly unacceptable results. Others, attempting to bypass theological and exegetical questions while concentrating upon practical matters, have not fared much better.
>
> The fact of the matter is that it is irresponsible and dangerous to attempt to do practical work apart from a sound theological base.[6]

Irresponsible? Dangerous? *Really?* Yes, really. Trying to perform the practical aspects of pastoral ministry without a proper theological foundation *is* irresponsible and dangerous, and it inevitably leads to serious problems within the church.

FOUR CONSEQUENCES OF THE SHIFT

Beyond the general consequences to the church already noted—decline in influence, failure to keep pace with population growth—several other "dangerous" consequences leap to mind. David Fisher had some of those dangers in mind when he declared:

> What is most curious to me is that evangelicals unquestioningly embrace nontheological ministry models. Some move the model to therapeutic and others to management models of ministry. In either case, evangelicals tend to think of both the church and ministry in human terms, an unreflective immanence. It is ironic that the liberal theological agenda that centered in anthropology and featured immanence is now implicitly championed by conservatives. The result is, more often than not, a failure of theological-biblical integration and, at the heart of it, a base for ministry that is not properly biblical or theological.
>
> Yet a pastoral ministry equipped and empowered for this generation must have a proper biblical and theological base. Methodology without a proper base is dangerous and ultimately powerless. In other words, we had better figure out our identity before we start dealing with the work of the church and the ministry in today's world. We dare not form pastoral roles based on human models, or we will accomplish little for God.[7]

I want to accomplish all that I can for God. I don't want to manage only a "little," if greater things are possible. But accomplishing little for God is just one of the dangers of trying, in Adams' words, "to do practical work apart from a sound theological base." There are, in fact, countless others.

In view of space limitations, I will confine myself to four of the most pernicious.

1. Loss of Enthusiasm Leading to Pastoral Burnout

Those who enter the ministry apart from a sound biblical and theological foundation are setting themselves up for a fall. People generally go into the pastorate because they have a strong desire to pastor. But often when they get there, they find that the existing forms and structures and expectations of the church quickly douse their enthusiasm and eventually prompt them to lose sight of their original goal. Ultimately, they burn out.

Entering ministry with a solid biblical base does not exempt anyone from the stresses, disappointments, and traumas common to ministry, but it does provide a rock-solid floor to stand on when the walls come crashing down. A person with only a sackful of skills in hand is much more likely to bolt and run from a difficult ministry than is the person who grips tightly the promises and instruction of Almighty God.

2. Disappointment Caused by a Misunderstanding of the Pastorate

On the other hand, some earnest Christians enter the pastorate because someone sold them a vision of ministry not based on a solid theological foundation. It often happens as follows: A person unsure about which vocational track to pursue takes a gifts and talents analysis to gain insight into where he or she "fits." The test indicates the person has the character traits to make a good counselor or social worker ... or, in the religious arena, a good pastor. The "experts" say, "Look, you could be a social worker or a counselor or a pastor." And that's that. Pastorate, here we come.

Is it any wonder that many pastoral candidates leave the ministry so quickly? Without a deep and genuine sense of calling (see chapter 8) or a broad understanding of and appreciation for the pastoral role as defined by God's Word, all too many of us lack the sense to avoid the demanding life of a biblical shepherd—and, of course, the church suffers in the process.

3. Loss of a Central Focus on God

When we cut loose a biblical anchor in one ocean, we tend to begin drifting in other seas as well, not only from force of habit but because such an approach is consistent. For example, once church leaders began to emphasize the "practical" aspects of ministry and to minimize the "theological" ones, it was no great leap to begin emphasizing the "practical" elements of life over the "theological" ones.

I saw this up close and personal in one of the churches I pastored. The disciples of a certain professor criticized me for not being seeker-sensitive enough. "You need to take a verse and hit a felt need," they lectured me. "You preach too much on the holiness of God and 'highbrow' theological subjects like that." Whether or not they realized it, they were asking me to focus more on people and less on God.

Since that time, I have been greatly helped and encouraged by John Piper's excellent book *The Supremacy of God in Preaching*. His work liberated me by helping me develop a sound theology for what I believe a pastor ought to be doing. Piper does not champion a pragmatic approach to preaching![8] Rather, he argues that, somewhere along the line, *we have to show them God*.

George Barna, who has dedicated his career to helping the church become all God wants it to be, has written:

> Faith used to revolve around God and His ordinances and principles; the faith that arrests our attention these days is that which revolves around us. We have demystified God, befriended Jesus, abandoned the Holy Spirit, and forgiven and even warmed up to Satan. Few Americans possess a sense of awe, fear, or trembling related to God.[9]

When was the last time you heard a contemporary pastor preach on God's holiness or lift up the great themes of God's attributes? I don't even hear much talk about passion for God these days. Students in many of our seminaries' homiletics courses are told to stay away from those themes because people don't want to hear about them any longer.

Yet preaching on God's character is at the heart of getting to know and love him, and it is the only thing that creates holy passion for godliness and truth and loving relationships. We'll continue to be in trouble until we restore that dimension of church practice.

Of course, I'm not talking about a mere intellectual recitation of God's attributes and works, an arm's-length, dispassionate, sterile, objectified, bloodless, and endless droning on about the crucial differences between infralapsarianism and supralapsarianism. Rather, we must so live and walk with the Savior that when we open our mouths to preach about him, the words that proceed from our lips not only bring light to the minds of our hearers but glowing warmth to their hearts. We should preach about the mighty themes of God not to tickle imaginations, but to inflame and ennoble hearts; not to help our hearers pass a written test, but to equip them to pass on a living faith.

4. Loss of a Working Ecclesiology

Os Guinness has rightly but sadly observed:

> Today theology is really no more than marginal in the church growth movement at the popular level. Discussion of the traditional marks of the church is virtually nonexistent. Instead, methodology is at the center and in control. The result is a methodology only occasionally in search of a theology. After all, church growth ... is a self-professed "science," not a theology.[10]

What Guinness wrote regarding the church-growth movement is equally true of the evangelical church at large. A profound lack of "theologizing" about the pastoral role has resulted in an equal silence on the nature of the church, much to our corporate detriment.

It is thrilling to realize that God has always had a people—but what are the identifying marks of that people? Who has God placed over them, and to whom has he entrusted the responsibility of caring for them? How can God's people come to know him more fully? How are they to behave toward those who don't yet know God in a personal way? What effect are God's people to have on their society? How is this impact to be made? How is it not to be made? These are all questions of ecclesiology. Unfortunately, answers are few and far between today.

David Fisher has pondered deeply our lack of vigorous theologizing about the church, and he has reached some hard but helpful conclusions:

> American Protestant theology has for some time been more interested in matters of polity than fundamental ecclesiology. American ecclesiological thinking tends powerfully toward matters of organization, polity, offices, and officers. Definition is important but seldom gets beyond the nature of the universal church or, at the local church level, the meaning of the word *ecclesia*. In the Bible, however, the doctrine of the church is far larger and profoundly deeper. Biblical ecclesiology features the distinguishing *character* of the people of God.... Of what value is theology if it does not point in some way to the local church where faith and life occur? Does anyone remember that the New Testament is written to churches?[11]

Indeed. Yet we continue to neglect the rigorous thinking and biblical theologizing about the church that can help us—really help us—to become the mighty tool in God's hands that we were intended to be. Fisher continues:

> Because of neglect, the practice of the church has become ecclesiology. Most ecclesiological conversation and theol-

ogy is largely descriptive. There doesn't seem to be a lot of biblical and theological reflection about the local church. The stakes are quite high, especially if ecclesiology in a very real way is the place where all theology finally rests. The implications for a church and its ministry are enormous.[12]

It is because of this that many years ago I helped to found the Seminary of the East. For several weeks we wrestled and debated about the proper place to begin our students' course of study. Should it be theology proper or ecclesiology? In the end, ecclesiology won out. We wanted our students to think deeply about what it means to be the people of God, to consider carefully their role and responsibility in the midst of God's people. Without a defined theology, we will have a defective ministry. Therefore, every pastor must be a pastoral theologian.

GOD DEFINES WHAT HE ORDAINS

Where do you begin if you want to become a pastoral theologian? How do you start? I begin like this: *If ministry belongs to God, then God should define what ministry looks like and what the role of pastor is to be.* Anyone considering the pastoral ministry must start with the Word of God. Our philosophy of ministry must be founded on a biblical theology. Unless we build out of the Scriptures our theology of what it means to be a pastor, we'll miss the whole thing.

I can't tell you how many philosophy of ministry papers I have read over the years, both from those applying for church staff positions and from those seeking an adjunct teaching slot, that included absolutely *no* theological foundation whatever (although they sprinkled in a few Bible verses here and there). Yet that is the critical piece.

As my friend Larry Crabb often says, we need a theological grid to sift out the junk we encounter. If pastors do not develop a theology that informs their identity—what they are to be and do and what is rightfully expected of them—they will be driven by every wind of change that whistles into town. And frustration is the guaranteed result.

The best way to guard against being driven hither and yon by ever-changing gusts is to anchor one's ship to the never-changing Word of God. Joe Stowell, president of Moody Bible Institute, has accurately said:

> Function is clearly defined in Scripture and, unlike form, is never fluid. Power in ministry lies in its biblically prescribed functions. Form is merely the passage through which the power flows. If all the emphasis is on form, we will have a "form of godliness" without the power (2 Timothy 3:5). Too often we are led to believe that if we had the right forms we'd have the power. Ministry was never intended to be managed that way. The Spirit is poised to empower biblical functions (Acts 1:8; Matthew 28:18–20).[13]

The starting point for all of this? I believe it is God and his character. How has God chosen to reveal himself to us as the model of what a pastor ought to be and represent (see chapter 6)? We are to reflect God's character qualities as we see them pictured in the Scriptures.

David Fisher is dead on target when he writes:

> We must learn to take our cues from God as he revealed himself in Christ. While the changing culture does form a most significant part of our formation and function as pastors, our primary cues must not come from the culture. And though the churches we serve are subcultures with their own forms, styles, traditions, and expectations, the churches do not give us our orders. And although the professional world has much to offer the church and pastors in a rapidly changing world, management techniques dare not define the work of God's servants.[14]

I cannot stress enough how pivotal and radical this concept is for the church and for her pastors. We *must* learn to sift through a theological grid rather than a pragmatic one.

It is imperative that we get back to a pastoral theology rather than a practical philosophy. A pastoral theology seeks to define from the Scriptures the role of the pastor—and there is no better base for life and ministry and direction than the Scriptures. We must heed the words of those who remind us:

> We adapt to our culture as a matter of theological integrity, not merely because it works. The foundation of that kind of pastoral thinking is sociological and can produce nothing more than human power can generate. The results of any method cannot be greater than the method itself. We need something more.[15]

What we need is a revival of pastoral ministry as defined by Almighty God. The only proper basis for ministry and life is biblical and theological. God's Word is our necessary foundation. If we want the church to make a difference in our increasingly secular society, we cannot look to that society for instruction. The answers—*real* answers, *practical* answers—are still to be found only in God's Word.

SO WHAT IS PASTORAL THEOLOGY?

To this point I have pleaded for the church to develop a sound, evangelical, pastoral theology. But what exactly have I been pleading for? What is a pastoral theology?

Seward Hiltner states that "pastoral theology is a formal branch of theology resulting from study of Christian shepherding.... It is just as important as biblical or doctrinal or historical theology, and ... it is no less the concern of the minister of the local church than of the specialist."[16] To further define pastoral theology, he explains, "Pastoral theology is ... that branch or field of theological knowledge and inquiry that brings the shepherding perspective to bear upon all the operations and functions of the church and the minister, and then draws conclusions of a theological order from reflection on these observations."[17]

I especially like Hiltner's emphasis on "shepherding." An effective pastoral theology must keep the model of the shepherd in the forefront. As Hiltner explains:

> Shepherding is in some degree present in everything done by pastor or church. A group meeting, a sermon, or a letter may contain as much shepherding intent and effect as does a bit of personal counseling. The notion of tender and solicitous concern that is behind the metaphor is in some measure to be seen as present in everything done by pastor and church, if these are rightly done. The view of shepherding as a perspective enables us to think of shepherding as a readiness, an attitude, or a point of view that is never absent from the shepherd and is therefore in some way involved in all his feelings and actions.[18]

A more contemporary author has written:

> Pastoral theology is that branch of Christian theology that deals with the office and functions of the pastor. . . . Pastoral theology is also a form of systematic theology because it attempts a systematic, consistent reflection on the offices and gifts of ministry, and their integral relationship with the tasks of ministry. . . . To achieve a wise perspective, pastoral theology must not be artificially detached from homiletics, liturgics, or catechetics, as if these disciplines could go their own way without interacting with one another. Pastoral theology wishes to gather the kernels of their varied insights into a single, unified account of the pastoral office. . . .
>
> Pastoral theology is dependent upon, and intrinsically connected with, each of the disciplines of the wider theological curriculum. As theology, pastoral theology wishes to bring exegetical and historical materials to bear on the theory and practice of ministry. It seeks to give clear definition to the tasks of ministry and enable its improved practice.[19]

In general, therefore, an adequate pastoral theology will exhibit at least the following characteristics:

- It is based solidly in Scripture.
- It considers "shepherd" its controlling metaphor.
- It interacts with and is informed by other theological disciplines.
- It guides pastors in the practical tasks demanded by their role.
- It helps pastors to think deeply and biblically about their identity and calling.

WHAT DOES PASTORAL THEOLOGY DO?

"That's fine," you might say, "but what specifically does a pastoral theology *do*?" That question came home to me in a profound way when I returned to seminary in an effort to finish an M.Div. program I had dropped years earlier to pastor full-time. I still remember one day as though it were yesterday—I was sitting in class, totally frustrated, and growing angry.

My professor and classmates were fervently discussing the decrees of God and the sovereign hand of the Lord, arguing with theologians who had ceased to breathe decades, even centuries, before—and I thought of the Scripture: "He still speaks, even though he is dead" (Hebrews 11:4).

But after a while, I just couldn't take it any longer. "Wait a minute," I said. "I have a couple in my church who just had a stillborn baby. Two weeks before that, a twenty-one-year-old died of cancer, and three weeks before that, a nineteen-year-old was killed in a car accident." I looked around and heard myself saying, "So tell me about the decrees of God and the sovereignty of God."

Pastoral theology informs the other theologies. It brings the abstract into contact with the existential realities of life. Apart from the pastoral perspective, the others lose their edge. They become cold and hard and distant and objectified. Shepherds want to bring the abstract truths of God to bear on the existential realities of life.

It's true that God is sovereign, but how does that help me minister to the woman who just gave birth to a stillborn child? Simply quoting Romans 8:28 does not suffice in her desperate hour of need. God revealed himself to us through his Word for a reason. He did not do so merely so we could debate the extent of his decrees but so that we might know him and receive comfort, encouragement, even rebuke from him in the midst of life. That woman needed to know that God loved her. She needed to connect with him in the midst of her anger and bitterness. Outlining the differences between respected theologians was not going to help her. It is the role of pastoral theology to bring those lofty concepts of God to bear on real-life situations.

A friend of mine who pastors in Harlem once told me, "My need is not to argue about the intricacies of inerrancy, although I need to understand them. My need is to articulate to my people that God is God and that he has spoken to us through his Word, even when a twelve-year-old gets pregnant after being raped by a gang of kids. He is God even when the crack baby is born and gets handed to his grandmother. That's the reality of theology, the doctrine of God." Such a perspective does not minimize the importance of theological discussions. Rather, it recognizes that unless the pastoral perspective is maintained, our discussions lose their significance.

The center and focal point of all our theologizing ought to be a pastoral theology that keeps the other theologizing on track. Historical, systematic, and biblical theology won't naturally stay on track apart from constant interaction with poimenics, with shepherding God's flock.

Seminaries today probably spend more time on preaching, communication, counseling, and leadership skills than on anything else. Students graduate and have a pretty good idea about how to create change, how to build strategic plans, and the like. But how do such graduates know what to preach *on*? How will they know where a church should head, if such knowledge is not passed on to them in the form of a sound pastoral theology?

Or consider this. Why do American Christians, by and large, not evangelize? I think it's because we have based our rationale for evangelism on soteriology. "My neighbor doesn't know Jesus, so when he dies, he'll go to hell." Such a rationale may or may not motivate people (apparently, it doesn't motivate most of them), but what would happen if we linked evangelism not to soteriology—"I witness or people go to hell"—but to the character of God and his people—"I am so awed by God that I can't help but tell others how awesome he is"? I think the greatest motivator for world evangelization is based in the character of God and what it means to be his people, not the fact that someone who dies without Christ is going to hell. Hell is a reality, but it will impact me deeply only if I understand who God is and what he has called me to be as one of his people.

This isn't merely a theoretical argument, by the way. I know of some pastors, such as John Piper at Bethlehem Baptist Church in Minneapolis, who are doing exactly this. And where does such a perspective come from? It comes out of a pastoral theology that places ecclesiology and theology proper at center stage.

IS PASTORAL THEOLOGY OUTDATED?

Sometimes when I talk about this subject, some will roll their eyes and object, "But haven't we matured beyond the need for *shepherds*? I mean, come on! We're a modern, urban society. Most of us don't even own real wool sweaters, let alone know anything about the sheep from which the wool came. Glenn, poor boy, don't you recognize that science has brought us past these foolish, frivolous ideas? You can't really *believe* in this shepherd stuff, can you? Surely, you can't expect us, with our modern minds, to believe that God would want us to hold to these childish things of the past?"

Yes, actually, I do. In every generation some have used the idea of "progress" to defy or to abandon the models and principles God has given to us in his Word. Yet God does not change his mind or his tune. He says to us, much as he said to the ancient Israelites of Jeremiah's time, "Go ahead then, do what you think is best! But hear the word of the Lord: You *will* know whose word will stand—mine or yours" (cf. Jeremiah 44:25–26, 28).

You know what? God's Word is still standing!

But there is another way to look at it. Does compassion ever go out of style? Does genuine caring ever grow old? Can modern life ever do away with the basic human need to receive tender love? Do not all people of all times need a shepherd?

In my mind's eye, I can see Jesus moving slowly from town to village, "teaching in their synagogues, preaching the good news of the kingdom and healing every disease and sickness" (Matthew 9:35). And if I listen closely, I can hear Matthew weep tears of joy as he writes his next sentence: "When he saw the crowds, he had compassion on them, because they were harassed and helpless, like sheep without a shepherd" (v. 36).

Are people still harassed today? Are they still helpless? Do they need to receive the gentle, tender compassion of a loving shepherd?

Think of the people you know personally. Look at the men and women around you. Are any of them harassed? Helpless? Are any of them still wandering, still struggling, still hurting? My guess is, now more than ever—so they still need shepherds.

IT ALL DEPENDS ON THE FOUNDATION

Toward the beginning of his ministry Jesus told the "amazed" crowds a story about two home builders (Matthew 7:24–29). Although he called one man "wise" and the other "foolish," only one thing separated the two.

It wasn't the building materials.
It wasn't the blueprints.
It wasn't the landscaping.
It wasn't the workers.
It wasn't the weather.
It wasn't even the cost.

The only difference between these two men—the lone contrast—is that the wise man built his house on a rock, while the foolish man built his house on the sand. Everything looked fine for both men until a nasty storm hit. Then the wise man's home stood strong and tall despite the howling gale, but the foolish man watched his house splinter, collapse, and float away in jagged little pieces.

The right foundation is everything, whether you are building houses or ministries. You don't build houses on sand, nor do you build ministries on human ingenuity. You build both on the rock. Only then will both houses and ministries stand tall and strong when the storms hit.

Chapter 4

IT'S NOT ROCKET SCIENCE

Truly pathetic—that's what they were. The dregs of the National Football League. Described as "moribund" by *The New Encyclopaedia Britannica*, the 1958 Green Bay Packers posted a record of 1–10–1 and struck fear into no one's heart except those of their own fans. The Green and Gold had grown used to losing and expected nothing better of themselves.

That is, until Vince Lombardi.

Hired as head coach and general manager in February of 1959, Lombardi instituted immediate changes (some critics called them "Spartan" and "fanatical"), and in his first season led his team to a 7–5 record. But over the next eight years, the Packers won six divisional titles, five NFL championships, and the first two Super Bowls.

And it all began with a little speech that started off like this: "Gentlemen, this is a football...."

Lombardi emphasized the fundamentals. No, that's not quite right. He didn't merely emphasize them, he hammered them home with a ferocity and a bluntness seldom seen before. Quickly he became known throughout his organization (no longer moribund) and the rest of the league for his back-to-basics philosophy, a philosophy that was conveyed by quotes such as . . .

- "You never win a game unless you beat the guy in front of you. The score on the board doesn't mean a thing. That's for the fans. You have to win the war with the man in front of you. You have to beat your man."
- "It's not whether you get knocked down; it's whether you get back up."
- "Once you learn to quit, it becomes a habit."
- "People who work together will win, whether it be against complex football defenses or the problems of modern society."

George Halas, architect of the rival Chicago Bears, once said that "you might reduce Lombardi's coaching philosophy to a single sentence: In any game, do the things you do best, and do them over and over and over."

How did Lombardi's players respond to their coach? We can get a clue from former pro-bowler Forrest Gregg, who confessed, "When Lombardi said 'sit down,' we didn't look for a chair."

BACK TO THE BASICS

When Lombardi told the members of his new team, "Gentlemen, this is a football," he wasn't trying to embarrass them. He didn't intend to denigrate their intelligence or treat them like foolish children. Lombardi saw a team with great potential that desperately lacked one thing: If it was to win, it had to get back to the basics—and history shows he was right.

I think we are at a similar point in the history of the American church. We have tried this new approach and that innovative program, this exciting methodology and that fresh technique, but still we are mired in a losing season. What should we do? I think we should listen to Coach Lombardi and hurry back to the basics.

The way some people talk today, you would think that building an effective ministry takes the training and intelligence of a rocket scientist. But it doesn't! God hasn't made ministry complicated, though it may, at times, be very hard. The basics of the ministry are actually quite simple.

What are they? Jesus Christ is the Good Shepherd, we are his sheep, and God has appointed certain individuals to shepherd his sheep under the authority of the Good Shepherd. That's basically it. It may take an entire library to flesh out the implications of those basics, but in essence, that's what ministry comes down to. Our problem is that we have tried to run scores of complicated "plays," but no one has sat us down to say, "This is the church. If you are a pastor, this is who you are, this is what you do, and this is what you don't do." If God were to give us a "Gentlemen, this is a football" speech, he'd probably say, "Be shepherds of God's flock that is under your care" (1 Peter 5:2).

Yet we seem to prefer more complicated schemes and playbooks as big as Nebraska. It reminds me of my high school football team. One year a new coach who loved intricate blocking schemes and complicated plays took over our program. We spent weeks working on his new system . . . and lost our first two games badly. To his credit, our new coach recognized the disaster-in-the-making and said, "OK, we're going to go back and do straight-on blocking; we're going to cut the playbook in half." We ended up winning our division.

In more recent football history, the University of Oregon went from "Gang Green" to the bottom of the Pac 10 in defense when the school brought in a coach from the

Canadian Football League who instituted "the Edge" defense, in which players were instructed to back off the line. What a disaster! The Ducks forgot all the basics and went from Gang Green to just plain gangrenous.

Sure, it was probably fun (for awhile) for Oregon boosters to talk about "the Edge." My high school buddies and I had fun saying we had all these pulling tackles to do this and that. But the bottom line was, it didn't work and it wasn't necessary to win in our league—and I don't think it is necessary to be that complicated to win in the kingdom, either.

Numerous talented teams have lost because they forgot the basics and tried to run schemes beyond their abilities. Someone sold them a bill of goods that they couldn't get to the championship game unless they knew how to do this or that: "What you need is a passing game." "What you need is a running game." "What you need is a passing *and* a running game." "What you need is a fast back." "What you need is a big back." But the truth is that the teams that usually win are the ones that come back to, "This is a football. You keep this guy from getting that guy."

So it is in the church. God tells us, "Pastors, this is the church. You are a shepherd. That is the model under which people will grow and flourish. If you are going to fulfill my purpose, here's what you do: Feed them, tend them, protect them, discipline them. It's really pretty simple." The goal is to bring God's people into an ever-deepening relationship with their Lord and with one another in his family. When we shepherd the flock of God as God instructs us, the sheep are brought to maturity and authenticity.

Coach Lombardi knew that his players would enjoy success only when they gained a sound grasp of the basics. His famous speech, "Gentlemen, this is a football," reminds us that the church will likewise prosper and grow only as it firmly grasps the basics.

SUBTRACTION BY ADDITION

Human beings naturally tend to complicate the simple, especially as time goes on. Visitors to the Museum of Art in Chicago can see an example of this almost immediately after walking through its massive doors. The museum houses a stunning collection of military armor representing several centuries of human warfare. It's worth a visit to the museum just to see this collection. As you walk down the center corridor, admiring the displays, you amble through world history from one bloody century to the next. And as you walk, you begin to notice something. The more recent the armor, the more ornate, cumbersome, and heavy it gets.

Early armor consisted largely of contoured sheets of steel or mail designed solely to protect one's vital organs. Later armor erupts into intricate designs, adding nobs, hangars, and attachments for this weapon or that shield. Eventually, knights in full suits of armor had to be hoisted with block and tackle onto their equally encumbered steeds.

I suspect that this ornamentation frenzy would have continued its gaudy evolution forever, except for one thing. Near the end of the museum's armor collection hangs a single iron shield, exactly like an earlier one except for a new feature protruding from its center: a primitive pistol. With the invention of the gun, armor soon went the way of the dodo. No use in decorating your steel suit if it's going to double as your coffin. Funny, isn't it, what it sometimes takes to get us back to the basics?

But enough about war and weapons. Let's talk cars. I hate to say it, but they ruined the Thunderbird. What a sleek and stylish machine it was at the beginning! It could turn a head a quarter mile away without even trying. But then designers started adding things to it—fins, chrome, and everything else under the sun—until it looked like anything but a Thunderbird. Eventually the car became a grandiose, expensive monstrosity that didn't remotely resemble the heart-stealing piece of Americana it was in its youth.

But the worst offense wasn't that they added all these useless doodads to the Thunderbird. Rather, they made it into something else entirely. They kept calling it a Thunderbird, but they changed the basic car that it was. They started emphasizing a side feature and treated it as the central feature. So in the end, it wasn't just a car with a fin. Instead, they started treating the fin as if it were the whole car.

Not to pick on Ford, but I also think of the blessed Mustang. The longer it stayed around, the bigger and uglier it became. When Ford finally got around to redesigning it several years ago, some smart engineers went back to the original "Stang's" 1964 roots and developed a monster of an automotive hit. Something similar is happening with the "new" VW Bug (and even with my beloved Chevy Corvette!).

There's a lesson in all this that we apparently need to relearn every so often: Leave the basics and lose. Return to the basics and win.

Now, I'm not pleading for a return to eighteenth-century ministry styles or eleventh-century ministry forms or even first-century ministry structures. Many of the specifics of ministry necessarily change through the years, and it's neither wise nor even possible to try to "freeze" the operation of the church in any particular era. Certain groups have tried to do that—the Amish, for instance, or the Russian Old Believers—but it doesn't really work. It can't. Times change, and so must the church.

But what *never* changes are the basics. At the heart of ministry, in God's viewpoint, are sheep and shepherds—always. We forget that to our own detriment.

Why is it, I wonder, that esteemed pastors from days gone by, such as Charles H. Spurgeon, could shepherd thousands of men and women in a time long before e-mail and faxes and telephones and pagers and cell phones? They didn't just show up to preach and teach on Sunday. Historians inform us that Spurgeon spent hours after the services ministering to his flock. Sundays saw a steady stream of people coming through his study. He spent the rest of the week either training his pastors or studying, but he always made time for his people. Why? Because Spurgeon understood the basics. He knew God had called him to be a shepherd and that his sheep needed attention. So he gave it to them. It's that simple.

SIMPLE DOESN'T MEAN EASY

Do not think, however, that simple and easy are the same thing! I would be the last person to claim that ministry is easy. I know better! At least three realities of ministry make it difficult from time to time.

1. Some Sheep Come After Us.

Not all sheep are loving; not all sheep bring us joy. Some nip at our heels and ram us when our backs are turned, not just once but year after year. Other sheep want to run, while still others constantly look in other folds, convinced that the grass must be greener over there. (Erma Bombeck once observed that the grass is greener only over the septic tank!)

All of these things can give us headaches, stomachaches, or worse. Ministry is not "easy." But our call remains simple and straightforward: "Be shepherds of God's flock that is under your care."

2. The Role Can Be Emotionally Draining.

Just the other day I was talking to a man about his disintegrating marriage. As he told me what was happening between him and his wife, it seemed clear to me what needed to take place. Even simple. We needed to sit both partners down, confront them on several issues of sin and lack of repentance, and challenge them to receive help from the body. It was a "no-brainer."

But the application of that process—now, that's a different story! That was terribly difficult. Nobody likes confrontation. We spent several days before our meeting praying about what to say, thinking it through. On several occasions, one of the spouses became suicidal. We discovered that the implementation of God's "simple" remedy was, in fact, terrifically difficult on several levels: emotionally, spiritually, and personally.

Yet God's plan for me as pastor was clear. If I cared about the sheep, then I had to help my sheep see their needs. Nevertheless, doing that was *tough*. One of the sheep accused some of those involved of being out to get him, of not being loving, of not caring about him. That hurts when you know you *do* care. Yet God said that's what a shepherd does. Simple in one sense, complicated in application and implementation—and *hard!*

I know it would be a lot easier to run a program in which everything is cut-and-dried and fits into neat little boxes. But real shepherds don't get to work with a lot of neat little boxes. Ministry to people tends to be much messier than that.

Suppose you place a man who's been involved in immorality under church discipline. You bring together a spiritual care team to walk with him through the process. Often the first thing everyone who knows the man wants to hear is, "What are the timelines? When is he going to be completely restored?" As a shepherd you have to say, "I don't know." Your commitment is to walk with that man through the process of restoration. It's not a program. You can't say, "Do your homework, memorize the verses, finish the curriculum, go through the counseling, and in fifteen weeks, you'll be restored and we'll move on to other issues." Granted, that would be a lot easier on our emotions. But life doesn't usually work out that way.

Have you ever seen those flowcharts on church discipline and restoration? They can be helpful, but real lives don't usually follow the paths depicted on the charts! The charts say, "If the person repents, he advances to this box and does such and such, and then he is restored and brought back into full church fellowship." The problem is, often a person will repent, then sort of "unrepent," then leave, then return.... In my experience, dealing with human lives looks more like a jigsaw puzzle than a flowchart—and jigsaw puzzles, though conceptually simple, can be extremely difficult to assemble.

3. The Demands of Modern Life Complicate Ministry Tasks.

Although ministry at its root is not complicated, its related tasks are growing ever more complex. Human resource laws, tax-reporting regulations, accounting requirements, IRS codes, legal changes, personnel issues, retirement plans, and the like all work together to make ministry much more complex than it was even a century ago. Ministry can become complicated, and ever increasingly so, especially as a church grows.

But ministry itself is not complicated. The essence of ministry is not complex. The nuts and bolts of pastoral ministry are not complicated. It still all comes down to, "This is a football." Television analysts might make the game out to be some version of rocket science, but it's not. Vince Lombardi proved that the game isn't all that complicated, as long as you stick to the basics. I think that's where we've messed up.

MAYBE WE DON'T WANT IT SIMPLE?

Ministry is not rocket science, but could it be that we wish it *were* more complicated than it is? Is it possible that we really *want* some other, more complex, model?

I titled chapter 2 of this book "The Neglected Model," but I wonder if the shepherd metaphor isn't so much neglected as rejected. By and large, it seems to me that we have rejected the shepherd's role that God designed for the proper functioning of the church. Why? Perhaps because it is too different. It flies in the face of the world's approach to business. The shepherd model elevates (even boasts of!) the things of God over those of humans. It crucifies the flesh so that the spirit might live. It is deeply sacrificial. But in our flesh we have taken it on ourselves to redefine the pastoral role. Consequently, we lack the divine power we so frantically seek.

It's not the first time such a horrible event has occurred. It also happened during the days of Samuel centuries ago: "And the LORD told him [Samuel]: 'Listen to all that the people are saying to you; it is not you they have rejected, but they have rejected me as their king'" (1 Samuel 8:7).

Perhaps we have not rejected the Lord as our king, but we have, at least, rejected him as our guide. As long as we continue to neglect, spurn, or outright reject his vision for the church and its pastors, we can expect to struggle and see our influence continue to wane.

So why don't we always like the "simple"? Because the simple doesn't always bring us the comfort we seek. It might be the best way, the only way, but if it is not the most pleasant way, we kick and buck and search for another way.

When my son was little, I took him to a basketball training camp. Two nights a week, fathers brought their kids to the gym to learn how to play the game. My son, along with all the other sons and daughters there, pleaded to get behind the three-point line to heave the ball at the basket, even though, at eight or nine years old, they could hardly loft it half that distance with any hint of accuracy. Their instructor wouldn't let them do it. Instead, he patiently explained, "Now, this is how you hold the ball. This is where your elbow is supposed to be. This is where your feet are to be. Make sure your shoulders are squared to the basket. When you bring your hand up for a shot, I want you to release the ball just like you're waving good-bye as the ball comes off your fingertips."

The kids hated every bit of it. They despised it. My son argued with me every night. He wanted to stand out at the three-point line and throw the ball as hard as he could up at the rim. It was almost impossible to convince those kids that they would be able to make three-pointers only if they learned the basic, fundamental principles of basketball. Today, however, I love watching my son toss in three-pointers. Nothin' but net!

You know what? The same thing is happening in the church. We try to drop in three-pointers before we master ministry's basic, rudimentary principles. God did not design ministry to be rocket science. In his Word he tells us, "Here's how you stand. Here's how you hold the ball. And when you learn to do it right, guess what? You're going to score a whole bunch of points."

FORCED DEPENDENCY UPON THE GOOD SHEPHERD

The essence of ministry is simple, but not easy. When it gets difficult, all of us can admit to thinking, "Okay, God, if you're the ultimate Shepherd, then why did you allow this sheep in here?" We know that God could have planted that person, that sheep, in anyone's fold—but he or she is in ours. Why? I think it's so that we ask, "Is there something here that I need to learn? Is there something that the rest of the sheepfold needs to learn through this person and this process?"

Dealing with human lives according to the biblical model of shepherding throws all of us out of our comfort zones, out of our depth. It forces us to rely on the Chief Shepherd. It forces us back into a position of utter dependency on God in a way that the corporate model simply doesn't.

I often remind myself and my staff that unless God moves a sheep someplace else, we are his choice to minister to that sheep. Maybe we wish we could sell them for mutton, but we can't. A rancher could, but not a shepherd—and that's what we've been called to be. It's really that simple.

ROCKET SCIENTISTS RETURN TO THE BASICS

Even rocket scientists know that success often depends on getting back to the basics. Recently scientists at NASA developed a machine to test the strength of the windshields used in airliners, military jets, and the space shuttle. They developed a gun to launch dead chickens at maximum velocity against the windshields to simulate high-altitude collisions with birds.

When British engineers heard about the gun, they eagerly arranged to use it to test the windshields of their new high-speed trains. But the Englishmen were appalled when they fired the gun, for the chicken shattered the windshield, crashed through the control panel, snapped the engineer's backrest in two, and imbedded itself in the back wall of the cabin. Hurriedly they sent NASA the specifications of the windshield and the horrifying results of their experiment, begging the rocket scientists for suggestions. NASA sent back a one-sentence response: "Thaw the chicken."[1]

Like these engineers, pastors encounter disastrous results when they forget the "basics" of what they are doing. I don't believe that ministry is rocket science. God has said to us, "I've given you your mission, your vision, and your strategic plan: Be shepherds of my flock. You start in Jerusalem, head to Judea, then move on to Samaria and the uttermost parts of the world. And keep shepherding until everyone has been reached or I return" (see Acts 1:8).

Part 2

CALLING ALL SHEPHERDS

Chapter 5

WHO AM I?

P astor, I can't take it anymore. I think my marriage is over.
I don't know what she wants or expects, and it's driving
me nuts! Every time I turn around, she's read another
book or heard another famous speaker—and I'm supposed
to change to fit her new mold. I'm no Frank Sinatra, but I've
gotta be me!"

I can't tell you how many times I've heard this or something similar in my counseling appointments. I usually
respond by trying to help such men understand their identity in Christ and who God has called them to be.

The great irony is that I've heard almost identical statements from pastors—not about their marriages, but about
their ministries! "Glenn, I can't take it any longer. I think my
ministry is over. I don't know what they want me to be: a
leader? a manager? a preacher? a counselor? a fount-of-all-
wisdom? I know God called me into the ministry, but I'm
not sure what the ministry is any longer—and I certainly
don't feel as though I measure up."

We all lose effectiveness when we lose our identity.
Without a strong biblical identity, we are tossed to and fro
by every changing wind. That's just as true of pastors as it

is of anyone else. If we lose sight of what it means to be a pastor, if we lose our identity as shepherds of God's flock, our ministries will inevitably flicker, fade, and die like a candle deprived of oxygen. When we lose that "shepherd focus," frustration and ineffectiveness inevitably result. On the other hand, when we rediscover that focus and hang on to it with all the strength our Chief Shepherd gives, we find a massive source of strength that enables us not only to succeed in ministry, but to thrive.

I count myself incredibly blessed to have been able to study and to be mentored by a number of wise pastors— seasoned, experienced, clear-eyed shepherds. From my earliest days of training and equipping, it was ingrained in me that I was to shepherd and mobilize the people of God. The Lord never called me to be everything to everyone; he never asked me to become an ecclesiastical jack-of-all-trades.

I am a pastor, a shepherd of the sheep, and anything that diminishes that role must be delegated to people called, gifted, and equipped for that function. That's why, in my first pastorate, I asked a musically gifted man to lead worship. "But our pastor has always led the worship," he replied. "Yes," I said, "but first, I don't have a good singing voice, and second, you do. Third, you love to lead worship, so I'd like you to take this over, if you are willing."

This is part of what it means to function as a body. One of our main tasks as pastors is to mobilize our sheep in their areas of giftedness and calling. At larger churches my task has not been to find someone to lead worship or to direct the children's ministry but to help the church see that my role is that of a pastor, not a CEO. My fundamental role and identity does not change just because I move from a church of one hundred to a church of three thousand. Even though I can't spend time every week with every individual in the church, I never want to lose my focus as a shepherd of God's sheep. While I cannot be everyone's personal pastor,

I must always retain my identity as the shepherd. I am not primarily a manager or a leader or a CEO or a facilitator or a commander or a counselor or any of a thousand other possibilities. God has called me to be a pastor, to shepherd the flock he has placed under my care, and the only way I can fulfill that holy calling is by keeping focused on my biblical role.

WE MINISTER OUT OF OUR IDENTITY

I am convinced that many of us struggle with ministry because we have no clear idea of who we are as pastors. All of us function out of a sense of identity, but if we are not clear on that identity, we're in big trouble.

I also believe that when people (including pastors) seek to minister outside of their identities, no amount of gimmicks can compensate. Without a firm sense of who we are and what we are called to do, we'll just spin our wheels, blindly following every fad that comes along—with frustration and ineffectiveness as our constant, unwelcome companions.

David Fisher made this unpleasant discovery when he took his first pastorate. He writes:

> I learned there is little satisfaction in performance of task without a clear and foundational identity. Nothing in seminary prepared me for this identity crisis. I knew who I was at 11 o'clock Sunday morning. My evangelical roots and training were certain that in the act of preaching I was God's herald, proclaiming God's Word in power. But who was I the other 167 hours of the week? I certainly didn't walk around town preaching continually.[1]

Later Fisher adds:

> For a Christian, the question of identity is far more than a psychological issue. If our struggle is merely our psychological loss of significance, the answer will be strictly human and will come in the form of therapy or

some sense of higher self-esteem. That is no answer to people who are created by God and made new by Christ. Our identity must be filled with Christian content—that is, rooted in God, formed by Christ, and empowered by the Holy Spirit.

For Christian pastors, the question of our identity is far deeper than professional models or cultural adaptation. It is certainly more than regaining some of our lost respect from the culture or the church. Our identity, our sense of calling, our mission in life must be grounded in Scripture and filled with theological integrity.[2]

In other words, who we *are* determines what we are to *do*. Consider the implications that different identities have for our ministry priorities:

- If God has called us to be leaders, then our priority becomes goals, objectives, and the bottom line.
- If God has called us to be managers, then our priority becomes structure, systems, order, and keeping everything under control.
- If God has called us to be CEOs, then our priority becomes developing a vision and issuing directives.
- If God has called us to be shepherds, then our priority becomes caring for, feeding, and correcting the sheep.

You can't do it all. Neither can I. No one can. So the first question we must answer is: What has God called us to be? What is our God-given identity? Everything else will flow from our answer to that question.

WHO DOES GOD SAY WE ARE?

Scripture uses various terms and images to describe the people whom God uses. The Lord calls us "servants" (Matthew 24:45), "workers"(Matthew 9:37), "stewards" (1 Corinthians 4:1, KJV), "managers" (Luke 12:42), "priests"

(Revelation 1:6), and even "kings" (1 Corinthians 4:8) and "royalty" (1 Peter 2:9). Richly descriptive as those terms may be, however, I do not think they best capture the identity of the pastoral role. Why not? Because they describe all believers, not pastors in particular.

So what terms *does* Scripture use to describe pastors and those in church leadership? Here again, we find a variety of terms. We read often of "elders," "overseers," "teachers," "prophets," and "leaders."[3] We also encounter the metaphors of "soldier," "athlete," and "farmer,"[4] and once the church's leaders are called "pillars."[5]

It is, of course, both biblical and legitimate to think of the pastoral role in any of these terms. But one central question remains: When God addresses us specifically as pastors, how does he picture our role? Is there ever a time when God says to us, "Pastors, here is your governing model"?

I contend that there is. Peter—the "rock," the "pillar," the "apostle"—lays it out for us in 1 Peter 5:1–4. In that crucial text, one image rises above all others to help us define our biblical role:

> To the elders among you, I appeal as a fellow elder, a witness of Christ's sufferings and one who also will share in the glory to be revealed: Be shepherds of God's flock that is under your care, serving as overseers—not because you must, but because you are willing, as God wants you to be; not greedy for money, but eager to serve; not lording it over those entrusted to you, but being examples to the flock. And when the Chief Shepherd appears, you will receive the crown of glory that will never fade away.

Peter entreated his pastoral readers to be *shepherds of God's flock*. He didn't urge them to be priests or kings or leaders or managers or even servants. He vigorously appealed to them to be shepherds.

Granted, Peter does call these men "elders," urging them to serve as "overseers" and warning them against acting as "lords." But he *emphasizes* their role as "shepherds." He tells them to be "shepherds of God's flock that is under your care" and to be "examples to the flock." To complete this image in the strongest way possible, Peter reminds them that one day Jesus Christ, whom he calls "the Chief Shepherd," will reappear on earth to present his faithful shepherds with a "crown of glory that will never fade away." As far as Peter is concerned, there can be no more compelling image than that of the shepherd.

Of course, when Peter focuses our attention on the model of shepherd, he is drawing on a treasure trove of scriptural references, especially in the Old Testament. Further, he isn't the only New Testament writer to see the central importance of pastor-as-shepherd. Listen to the apostle Paul addressing the elders of the church at Ephesus in Acts 20:28–29:

> Keep watch over yourselves and all the flock of which the Holy Spirit has made you overseers. Be shepherds of the church of God, which he bought with his own blood. I know that after I leave, savage wolves will come in among you and will not spare the flock.

As before, these leaders are called "elders" and "overseers," but they are commanded to behave as "shepherds." Paul seems to think of "elder" and "overseer" more or less as job titles, but he urges these men to adopt "shepherd" as their central model of ministry. We must distinguish between form and function, though we often confuse the two. One could represent Paul's distinction between the two as follows:

Their position (form): Elder and overseer
Their identity (function): Shepherd

If, then, it is true that God wants us to find our basic ministry identity as shepherds, the next question to consider is, Why? Why did God choose the model of a shepherd? He could have chosen any number of models. Why not king or commander or general? Why not manager or leader or steward? Why did God use the model of a shepherd to define the role of the pastor?

I don't believe God uses terms flippantly. There must be something within the image of a shepherd that ought to capture and hold our hearts and imaginations, something that will keep us on track and galvanize our determination.

So what is it? Why does God want us to find our pastoral identity in the image of the shepherd?

WHY GOOD SHEPHERDS MAKE GOOD PASTORS

Let's start by remembering that even the English term *pastor* comes from the Latin word for "shepherd." The Latin verb *pascere* literally means "to put to pasture." Every time someone calls you "pastor," they're reminding you that God has called you to be a shepherd of the flock.

But what is so great about being a shepherd? Why is God so adamant that we behave as shepherds? Space won't permit me to go into much detail, but let me suggest five basic reasons why God instructs us to find our pastoral identity in the picture of a shepherd.

1. Shepherds Tend Sheep.

When God looks for a metaphor to describe his people, the term he most often chooses is "sheep." Consider just a few biblical examples:

Know that the LORD is God.
    It is he who made us, and we are his;
    we are his people, the sheep of his pasture. (Psalm 100:3)

We all, like sheep, have gone astray,
    each of us has turned to his own way. (Isaiah 53:6)

My people have been lost sheep;
    their shepherds have led them astray
    and caused them to roam on the mountains.
They wandered over mountain and hill
    and forgot their own resting place. (Jeremiah 50:6)

You my sheep, the sheep of my pasture, are people, and I
am your God, declares the Sovereign LORD. (Ezekiel
34:31)

When the Son of Man comes in his glory, and all the
angels with him, he will sit on his throne in heavenly
glory. All the nations will be gathered before him, and he
will separate the people one from another as a shepherd
separates the sheep from the goats. He will put the sheep
on his right and the goats on his left. (Matthew 25:31–33)

When Jesus landed and saw a large crowd, he had compassion on them, because they were like sheep without a
shepherd. (Mark 6:34)

I am the good shepherd; I know my sheep and my
sheep know me—just as the Father knows me and I
know the Father—and I lay down my life for the sheep. I
have other sheep that are not of this sheep pen. I must
bring them also. They too will listen to my voice, and
there shall be one flock and one shepherd. (John 10:14–16)

For you were like sheep going astray, but now you have
returned to the Shepherd and Overseer of your souls.
(1 Peter 2:25)

With all the animal metaphors available to the Lord—
horses, lions, eagles, bears, dogs, cats, cattle, fish—why does
he so consistently, in both Old and New Testament, refer to
us as sheep? If we look carefully at the biblical passages that
compare us to sheep, we can see several consistent features
(none of which are particularly complimentary):

- We stray like sheep.
- We need protection like sheep.

- We can be foolish like sheep.
- We require caretakers like sheep.

In short, the most obvious reason the Lord wants pastors to behave as shepherds is because the people entrusted to their care behave as sheep. Sheep need shepherds if they are to survive and thrive. Likewise, if we want the men and women, boys and girls in our congregations to survive and thrive, we must serve them as shepherds, not as CEOs.

2. Good Shepherds Are Absolutely Committed to Their Sheep.

God also instructs pastors to be shepherds to remind us to place our flock's interests above our own. Ezekiel 34 contains a blistering indictment of the "shepherds of Israel," those men God entrusted to take care of the Jewish people. God begins his rebuke with these stinging words: "Woe to the shepherds of Israel who only take care of themselves! Should not shepherds take care of the flock?" (Ezekiel 34:2).

Good shepherds are interested primarily in their sheep, not in schedules or programs or buildings or causes, as good and necessary as any of these may be. Jesus also called attention to this when he said:

> I am the good shepherd. The good shepherd lays down his life for the sheep. The hired hand is not the shepherd who owns the sheep. So when he sees the wolf coming, he abandons the sheep and runs away. Then the wolf attacks the flock and scatters it. The man runs away because he is a hired hand and cares nothing for the sheep. (John 10:11–13)

Of course, we pastors cannot lay down our lives for our sheep in the same way and for the same purpose as did our Lord, but we are expected to care deeply for the sheep entrusted to us—even when they're not easy to tend! Some sheep stray. Some refuse to be shorn (I'm told that they are called "woolie bogs" in the sheep industry). Some may even bite the shepherd or butt him when his back is turned.

Tell me ...

- How would a CEO react if an underling suddenly turned on him?
- How would a general respond if one of his soldiers refused an order?
- How would a king act if one of his subjects treated him with insolence?

It's not hard to imagine, is it? Perhaps that is why God (who knows sheep) instructs pastors to act as shepherds, not as CEOs, generals, or kings. God wants pastors who are truly committed to the sheep, not to their own interests or egos.

3. Good Shepherds Have Genuine Compassion for Their Sheep.

A third reason God chose the shepherd model has to do with the shepherd's heart. In Ezekiel 34 God charged Israel's "shepherds" with several crimes that teach us, through a negative example, what shepherds are *not* to be like:

- They took care of themselves instead of the flock.
- They did not strengthen the weak, heal the sick, or bind up the injured.
- They did not bring back the strays or search for the lost.
- They "ruled" the sheep brutally and harshly.

What was the result of this wicked dereliction of duty? The sheep "wandered over all the mountains and on every high hill. They were scattered over the whole earth" (Ezekiel 34:6). They were "plundered" and devoured by "all the wild animals" (verse 8). Therefore, God pledged to remove these shepherds from tending his flock and promised that he himself would care for his sheep by searching for and looking after them, by rescuing them from all the dark places they were scattered, and by leading them to good pasture. In fact,

God said, "I myself will tend my sheep and have them lie down.... I will search for the lost and bring back the strays. I will bind up the injured and strengthen the weak.... I will shepherd the flock with justice" (verses 15–16).

What a picture! While shepherds are forbidden to be brutal or harsh (except toward the predators), generals and kings and CEOs have no such restriction. Good and faithful shepherds look after their sheep, tend to their injuries, search for the lost, and bring them all to good pasture. Generals, kings, and CEOs are more concerned about the bottom line and ultimate results than they are about lost or hurting sheep. (Have you ever heard of a shepherd "downsizing" his flock?)

The picture God paints in Ezekiel 34 demands of pastors intense concern and devoted interaction, not dispassionate commands or distant strategizing. A general or a CEO or a king can (and oftentimes must) stay at a distance from his subjects, but a good shepherd must remain intimately connected to his sheep. And intimate connection with the flock is what God demands of those he calls to be pastors. That's one reason why God chose the image of the shepherd to define the role of the pastor.

4. Good Shepherds Need Courage to Defend Their Flocks.

It is no accident that the image of leader-as-shepherd blossomed in the Bible during the reign of David. This shepherd boy who later became the shepherd of Israel began his public career by rehearsing for King Saul his exploits as a literal shepherd: "Your servant has been keeping his father's sheep," he reported. "When a lion or a bear came and carried off a sheep from the flock, I went after it, struck it and rescued the sheep from its mouth. When it turned on me, I seized it by its hair, struck it and killed it. Your servant has killed both the lion and the bear" (1 Samuel 17:34–36).

As David's story shows, shepherds need courage. So do pastors of churches. When the apostle Paul told the

Ephesian elders, "I know that after I leave, savage wolves will come in among you and will not spare the flock" (Acts 20:29), he was reminding them not only of their duty to protect the flock but also of their need for courage in the face of attack. "Lions," "bears," and "wolves" cannot be confronted without courage, because it is the shepherd himself—not an employee or a messenger or an enlisted soldier—who is responsible to meet the attack.

No doubt Jesus had this in mind when he told the crowds, "I tell you the truth, I am the gate for the sheep. . . . Whoever enters through me will be saved. He will come in and go out, and find pasture" (John 10:7, 9). In ancient Israel, a shepherd literally functioned as the "door" to the sheep pen. Every night the sheep would be led into a sheepfold, and the shepherd would take his place in the single opening of the pen, even sleeping in that spot. If something wanted to get to the sheep, it would have to go through him—and to be such a door, my friend, takes courage.

We all want to be cared for. We want to know that we won't be deserted. People go from relationship to relationship because they're looking for true intimacy. They wander from job to job because they're seeking a sense of connectedness, purpose, and belonging. They hang out at clubs and bars because they want a place where everybody knows their name. The Chief Shepherd provides all those things they're looking for. He knows their name, and his sheep know his voice. He looks for them when they're lost, and he protects them from evil. Everyone wants a defender.

When Susan and I were first married, I had just come out of a somewhat angry and violent lifestyle. I struggled with the arguments put forward by Christian pacifists. Then one day I told Susan I was coming to the conclusion that even if someone broke into our home and attacked her, I would not be able to lift a hand against him. I will never forget the look on her face. She paused and, with horror written in her eyes, asked, "Even if someone was violating me, you would not stop him? What kind of a husband *are* you?" Her response took me aback. I still remember the look of fear on her face, the surprise, the hurt, the shock. Immediately I started rethinking my position. I quickly realized I had just pulled her rug of protection out from under her. Her security was gone. I started thinking again about Christ and how he gave his life for the church (Ephesians 5:25). What did that mean? What does it mean to be a protector?

Soon afterwards we had a mild "situation"—and everything in me leapt to protect Susan. All my instincts to defend and guard came rushing to the surface. Since then, Susan has said she always feels safe with me.

People want that, and I believe it is the shepherd model that provides it. A shepherd helps the sheep feel safe. People run in a million directions, looking for security, safety, and protection. What Susan wanted is what everyone wants. People come to a church looking for those things. They need to feel safe, to know that if they are attacked, their shepherd will defend them courageously.

Does a CEO or a king or a general or a leader need this kind of "frontline" courage? Not usually. But a shepherd does—and so does a pastor.

5. Shepherds Are Humble People.

Think of a CEO, a king, a general, or a leader. Does the word *humility* leap to mind? Probably not. But it should when you think of a shepherd, which is another reason why God chose this model for us to follow.

In the social structure of the ancient world, shepherds were pretty much the lowest of the low. For example, Joseph counseled his brothers to identify themselves to Pharaoh as tenders of livestock rather than as shepherds, because "all shepherds are detestable to the Egyptians" (Genesis 46:34). Later, in New Testament times, the testimony of a shepherd was inadmissible in court because his words were considered unreliable.[6] Throughout the centuries of Israel's history, shepherds were despised.

What, then, are we to make of God's insistence that we who are called to be pastors should picture ourselves as shepherds of his flock? I believe this divine command is meant to keep us humble. If we think of ourselves primarily as leaders or big shots, it is easy to start looking down on those who follow us. After all, they are at the bottom of the pyramid atop which we rule.

Perhaps this is why many today talk about "servant-leaders." The term "leader," on its own, often causes people to develop swelled heads. Seminaries, seminar leaders, and leadership gurus see that and so prefix the word "servant," just to remind everyone of our Lord's strong directive in Matthew 20:25–27:

> You know that the rulers of the Gentiles lord it over them, and their high officials exercise authority over them. Not so with you. Instead, whoever wants to become great among you must be your servant, and whoever wants to be first must be your slave.

To be honest, the term "servant-leader" doesn't do much for me. I appreciate what it is intended to convey, but it reminds me too much of a George Carlin routine poking fun at silly word pairings such as "jumbo shrimp" and the like. And besides, I don't think it's necessary. "Shepherd" does just fine.

Shepherds are humble people by definition. They know they occupy a lowly social position. Their whole lives are dedicated to service. The shepherd's life is not his own; the needs of his sheep take priority. Leaders may find it difficult to do "nothing out of selfish ambition or vain conceit, but in humility consider others better than" themselves (Philippians 2:3), but a shepherd *must* live that way if he is to faithfully discharge his calling.

When we consciously remember that we are shepherds, we remain humble. But when we start thinking of ourselves as leaders, humility tends to evaporate—sometimes, along with our ministry.

HOW I BECAME A SHEPHERD

By the time I was sixteen, I knew God wanted me to become a shepherd of his sheep. My parents came to Christ at a Billy Graham crusade when I was about nine, and seven years later I was working at a Christian summer camp and knew God was calling me to be a pastor. I wrote a letter home telling my parents of my conviction, but by the end of that summer I had changed my mind.

For a few years I rebelled and went through some "purple haze" days, but at the age of twenty I recommitted my life to Christ. Guess what? The call was still there. I knew immediately that God wanted me to prepare for the ministry. I traveled with a Christian music group for a year, during which time I was thoroughly discipled. Then I headed off to Bible college and later transferred to a little Bible institute. The head of the school told me, "Glenn, the school isn't accredited, but if you come here, I'll teach you what I know about being a pastor." That was good enough for me.

After that I attended seminary. I spent a year there and then ended up pastoring my home church in Morrisville, Pennsylvania, where I served as the full-time acting pastor for three years. It was there that I cut my teeth in ministry. During that time the church deacons regretted that I hadn't finished seminary, so they encouraged me to work on my degree during the summers.

Then came a call from a small-town church in south New Jersey. I spent seven years there, during which time I finished a Ph.D. program from Oxford Graduate School of Dayton, Tennessee.

Shortly thereafter I became involved in the founding of the Seminary of the East, a school built around a mentorship model. The school focused on training and equipping pastors. It seemed like simple logic to me that the teachers best qualified to equip pastors were those who had pastored themselves.

My heart always has been in the church, but a few years ago while I was pastoring in Denver I was asked to help out a fledgling organization called Promise Keepers. Someone had heard that I knew how to start things and that I could minister to men. So I was asked to serve on the board of directors, then later to leave the pastorate in order to serve as the organization's first vice president. I accepted the invitation and worked hard to take the movement to a national and international level. I also helped develop training materials, seminars, and other resources.

But all the while I deeply missed pastoring.

My wife kept saying to me, "You miss pastoring so badly. Maybe now's the time to get back to it." Susan and I have been married twenty-three years, and she knows me well. She is also most comfortable when I am pastoring, because she loves the dynamics of the local church. What's more, Susan was right. I missed watching a congregation mature over the long term. I missed seeing people grow in Christ. In short, I missed my sheep.

So in 1997 I resigned from Promise Keepers to resume my shepherding duties, this time as the senior pastor at Calvary Church in Charlotte, North Carolina. I love it. This shepherd is back where he belongs.

A SHEPHERD'S "TYPICAL" DAY

What does ministry look like when undertaken from a shepherd's point of view? How does it differ from a CEO-pastor's perspective? Apart from the philosophical differences between the CEO model and the shepherd model, what practical, day-to-day differences can be noticed?

I know how it affects my own ministry. For example, I just finished a ninety-minute meeting with the vice-moderator of our elders. We spent most of our time together in prayer, petitioning the Lord on behalf of the church, his family, my family, the families of the congregation, and a few troubled people we know. We had a great time of shepherding and ministering to one another. Would a CEO-pastor take time for that? Probably not. But a shepherd *revels* in it.

Earlier today I made a couple of phone calls to individuals in the hospital, letting them know we cared for them and were praying for them, and expressing my joy that others in the church were also ministering to them. I also spent some time studying for my sermons this Sunday.

Tonight I will interact with all of our ministry staff in a budget training meeting. But I won't train anyone in budgeting! Instead, I'll talk about what it means to be the people of God, how important a cooperative spirit is, and how all of this will help us encourage one another and to spur one another on to love and good deeds. That is, after all, the rationale for the budgeting process and the financial policies that will be taught. We want to do all things to honor God, even budgetary tasks. I'll shepherd them in working together as the people of God, but I'm not going to teach about budgeting. Someone else with expertise in budgeting will do that.

On another night I'll speak with several hundred ministry leaders, elders, deacons, and small-group leaders. We'll discuss what it means to have a heart for people and ministry, and we'll encourage each other in God's work.

Every week I schedule several appointments with people I don't know well. I do so because I do not want to get locked into a certain group within the church and never touch anyone outside of that group. Last week, for example, I met with a childless couple in the process of determining whether God wanted them to adopt. I can't meet with everyone in the church, but I need to keep meeting with several people outside my normal circles. As a shepherd of God's sheep, I can't afford to lose sight of the people in my spiritual care.

Most CEO-pastors tend to work only with a small handful of people and never touch anyone beyond that. But as a shepherd, I want my sheep to understand that I care about them, that I love them, that they are the reason for my call.

A CEO will often say, "Hey, this is where the company is going. Get on board or get out." A CEO-pastor might meet with a childless couple, but only if it affects the bottom line. The pastors I know who have adopted the CEO model would never meet with them. "I meet only with elders," they explain—but how can you know what's happening in the midst of the sheep if you meet only with the elders?

When I walk down to the kitchen to thank volunteers for serving a meal to our senior citizens, I do so not because that's what good leaders do, but because my sheep have just done a good thing and need to be recognized and appreciated for it. I am an introvert, and I don't mix easily in large groups. It's not easy for me to go out and spend a lot of time with people—but if a shepherd wants to be faithful to his calling, that is what he does.

The shepherding model also affects my preaching. I believe that my sermons are less academic and more life-oriented than they would be under the CEO model, though no less intellectually stimulating. It makes all the difference in the world when I share real needs from the pulpit and people know that I've been involved in their lives. Because I stay in contact with my sheep, I have a pretty good feel for what's happening in the church and what's happening in people's lives. Because of that, I can shift gears pretty quickly when I need to.

For example, we recently offered a series on worship after we had discovered that a significant number of our people were struggling to understand what biblical worship was all about. Because this sermon series grew out of *need*, it had a tremendous impact on our congregation. It was one of those seasons of ministry when you can just feel the messages hit home. But if we had not been plugged into the flock, it never would have happened.

I don't think my schedule is any more hectic (because I meet with my sheep) than that of the pastor who says, "I'm the CEO of this church, and I do not have time to meet with people." All I have done is prioritize my schedule to allow me to touch people's lives—and I believe the flock notices and appreciates that fact.

A FEW OBJECTIONS ANSWERED

So what do you do when you see the legitimacy of the shepherd model and want to adopt it . . . but your church is stuck on something else?

Believe me, I have been in plenty of meetings where someone says, "Now, Pastor, you just don't understand sound business principles. We can't expect to grow if we're violating some basic laws of business." I know how intimidating that can be, especially when what is being advocated *is* true in the business world.

But that is not the issue here. Whether the statement is true or not, I don't stop being a pastor to take on some other identity. Nor do I apologize for being a pastor. Granted, I might become more effective at what I do by learning some basic business principles, but I will *never* be what the Lord calls me to be if I abandon my identity as pastor. First and foremost I am a shepherd of the flock of God—*and that must never be compromised.*

When pastors don't have a sound biblical identity, they end up being intimidated and almost ashamed when someone tells them something like, "You just need to understand strategic planning a lot better." While that may be true and while such things may help us become more effective pastors, they can never be allowed to take the place laid out for us in Scripture. The Word of God insists that we "shepherd the flock of God." It does not demand that we attend strategic planning sessions or take part in leadership seminars or get degrees in financial management. Those things may be helpful, but they're not central, contrary to what some may say. To hear them talk, a pastor needs a counseling degree, a law degree, an MBA (better yet, he should be a CPA)— and several theology degrees just for good measure.

Enough! The Bible alone dictates what is central, and it maintains we are to shepherd God's people.

We must build a grid of theology through which we read and study all issues. What passes through that grid can be utilized; what gets snagged must be thrown out. This is as true for pastors as it is for anyone else. If we pastors do not adopt a biblical identity, we will become insecure and apologetic and even embarrassed when we get hammered with this or that new "requirement" for effective ministry. The truth is, we are called as overseers to shepherd God's flock, equipping them to use their gifts to meet the needs of the body. A pastor can't and *doesn't have to* "do it all."

This is just as true for the pastor of a single-staff church as it is for one of a multiple-staff church. Both must build teams that allow people to release their gifts. Nothing in the Bible says that I can't pastor a church of forty people and still have a staff of three, all of them volunteers. I can work with them, equip them, give them areas of responsibility, and let them do the work of the ministry.

HOW CAN I SHIFT?

Any time we want to bring about change, we must take two critical steps. First, we must create or acknowledge dissatisfaction with what exists. And second, we must create a vision of what the future can look like. Both steps take constant communication and teaching. It can't be done in any other way. Unless a pastor commits to do that, he's not going to change anything.

Of course, this is difficult. It may require that we publicly repent of our past way of doing things. We may have to say, first to the church leaders and then to the church as a whole, "I have sinned against you by not shepherding you. I may have run things pretty well, but I haven't shepherded you as the Bible tells me to. I haven't been the pastor that I should be—but I want to be! And with your help and through the power of the Holy Spirit, I will be."

THE CRY FOR SHEPHERDS

Our people are crying out for shepherds.

They've had enough of leaders.

They've had their fill of CEOs.

They're sick to death of managers.

What people really want—and really need—are pastors who long to be shepherds of God's flock. People today yearn for loving shepherds who care for the sheep, not because they must, but because they are willing, as God wants them to be. And they are searching for gentle overseers who are eager to serve, not greedy for money and not anxious to lord it over the flock.

Are you eager to serve? Do your sails fill with strong gusts of wind whenever you think of shepherding God's people? Does your pastor's heart swell with gratitude when you look at the sheep under your care and realize that God Almighty has called you to this place and to this time and to these people? If so, then you know the absolute importance of heeding what one professor told me so many years ago: "Don't ever lose sight of what it means to be a pastor."

"Be shepherds of God's flock that is under your care," Peter tells us (1 Peter 5:2). "Be shepherds of the church of God, which he bought with his own blood," Paul reiterates (Acts 20:28). That is the pastor's identity, and we must never lose sight of it.

May the God of peace, who through the blood of the eternal covenant brought back from the dead our Lord Jesus, that great Shepherd of the sheep, equip you with everything good for doing his will, and may he work in us what is pleasing to him, through Jesus Christ, to whom be glory for ever and ever. Amen. (Hebrews 13:20–21)

Chapter 6

......

GOD'S PORTRAIT OF A SHEPHERD

......

D
r. Lynn Anderson, president of Hope Network, a ministry dedicated to coaching, mentoring, and equipping spiritual leaders for the twenty-first century, had just finished delivering a sermon in which he repeatedly referred to church elders as "shepherds." After his talk, a dear friend and member of his congregation cornered him to challenge his choice of terms.

"Why don't you find a better way to communicate this spiritual leadership idea?" the friend asked. "No one here knows anything about shepherds and sheep, especially the way all that stuff worked in the ancient world. That picture just doesn't connect with a modern church."

Anderson considered his friend's challenge carefully but soon realized that no modern metaphor was suitable. So he replied, "I can't find any figure equivalent to the shepherd idea in our modern, urban world. Besides, if I drop the shepherd and flock idea, I would have to tear about five hundred pages out of my Bible, plus leave the modern church with a distorted—if not neutered—view of spiritual leadership."[1]

I believe Dr. Anderson is right. Historically, whenever the church has chosen some picture other than shepherd to describe its primary concept of spiritual leadership, error and decline have soon followed. Something in the image of a humble shepherd apparently serves to guide our activities and safeguard our leadership from abuses.

It is remarkable that, although the Bible uses many images to describe leaders among God's people—stewards, farmers, architects, servants, to name a few—one image stands head and shoulders above the rest. Time and time again the Lord uses the metaphor of the shepherd to describe and illustrate what he expects of those whom he places in roles of church leadership.

In this chapter I would like to consider two questions: How does the Bible portray the work of a shepherd? And what can we learn from this scriptural portrait to help us in our own shepherding task? I believe that by fixing in mind this divinely chosen metaphor, we will secure both an effective model to emulate and a worthy target to shoot for in our own ministries.

I doubt that there's any better place to start our inquiry than with the Bible's portrayal of God as the Shepherd of his people. If we want to know what a shepherd looks like and what a shepherd does, we should begin by examining the brush strokes used by the Shepherd of Israel in his own self-portrait.

GOD AS SHEPHERD

Think about the terms *pastor* and *pastoral* for a moment. Both hearken back to a rich scriptural image that finds its beginning and end in God Almighty, the "Shepherd of Israel" (Psalm 80:1). The term *pastor* is filled with magnificent imagery and significance, especially because it connects in a fundamental way to the very character and attributes of God.

God is first termed a shepherd in the opening book of the Bible. In Genesis 48:15, the elderly shepherd Jacob calls the Lord "the God who has been my shepherd all my life to this day." Don't miss the significance of this initial reference! Jacob, that old deceiver and scoundrel, has reached the end of a life filled both with discord and tenderness, poverty and riches, happiness and deep sorrow. In his younger days he had wrestled with the Lord, both figuratively and literally, and had received a new name, Israel, to mark his slow spiritual growth.

Jacob knew what it meant to be a shepherd! He spent fourteen hard years in the fields working for his father-in-law in order to gain the hand of his lovely wife Rachel and then another six years building his estate. He later described those long years as follows: "The heat consumed me in the daytime and the cold at night, and sleep fled from my eyes. It was like this for . . . twenty years" (Genesis 31:40–41). Yes, Jacob knew all about the life of a shepherd. He boiled in the day and froze at night and quickly became an insomniac!

Yet at the end of his days he calls the Lord "the God who has been my shepherd all my life to this day." Jacob knew he had been a difficult sheep, prone to wander and to stumble over steep cliffs. But he also knew that God had been with him every step of his troubled way, guiding him with his staff, prodding him with his rod. Jacob knew he belonged to the flock of God because the same Shepherd who cared for him in his early days still cared for him as he faced the grave.

So confident was Jacob in his divine Shepherd that he bequeathed the same confidence to his son Joseph. On his deathbed, Jacob called all his sons to his side and there declared to Joseph that it was "the Shepherd, the Rock of Israel, . . . your father's God" who had helped his favored son and kept him strong through his betrayal by his brothers, his long years in prison, and his rise to power in the pagan land of Egypt (Genesis 49:24). From all indications, Joseph "got it."

No doubt the most famous of all the Old Testament descriptions of God as Shepherd is found in Psalm 23, where David proclaims, "The LORD is my shepherd, I shall not be in want" (verse 1). Others have written beautiful treatises on this beloved text, and it is not my intent here to offer a fresh exposition of the psalm. But I want to pause long enough to note the primary ways in which David compares God to a shepherd:

- He meets our needs (verse 1).
- He forces us to get rest (verse 2).
- He brings us into life-giving surroundings (verse 2).
- He gives us peace (verse 2).
- He rejuvenates us when we're drained (verse 3).
- He enables us to live holy lives, to his everlasting praise (verse 3).
- He comforts us when death approaches (verse 4).
- He disciplines and guides us (verse 4).
- He helps us win over great opposition (verse 5).
- He blesses us in ways that leave us breathless (verse 5).
- He fills us with confidence for this life and hope for the life to come (verse 6).

It is worth noting that both the rod and the staff mentioned in verse 4 are said to "comfort" David, the shepherd-king. The shepherd's rod, which was always larger than the staff, was used to fend off attackers, while the staff was used to guide and correct the sheep. That picture alone ought to give us pause! The Lord says to us here, "I don't use the rod on you; I use the rod on your enemies. I *will* use the staff on you because I love you, but the staff is not as intimidating as the rod."

In pondering this classic psalm, Jay Adams noted:

> The name "pastoral" is a uniquely Christian term that expresses a fundamental concept that is deeply embedded in every biblical portrayal of Christian ministry. The term refers to a rich scriptural figure that finds its beginning and end in God. He, who is the "Shepherd of Israel" (Psalm 80:1), ultimately demonstrated the meaning of His covenantal love as the Great Shepherd of the sheep by giving His life for them (John 10:11). The figure virtually bursts with significance, far more than didactic statements ever could express. Let us, therefore, try only to capture something of what it meant for David (a former shepherd) to write:
>
> "The Lord is my Shepherd; I shall not want" (Psalm 23:1), for in that great declaration lies all that is meant by "Pastoral Work." To help to understand this, reread the sentence this way:
>
> "The Lord is my Pastor; I shall not want" (Psalm 23:1).
>
> The Shepherd is the one who provides full and complete care for all of his sheep.[2]

Of course, Psalm 23 isn't the only psalm to call upon God as Shepherd. In Psalm 28:9 David cries out to God, "Save your people and bless your inheritance; be their shepherd and carry them forever." Likewise, in Psalm 80:1, Asaph pleads, "Hear us, O Shepherd of Israel, you who lead Joseph like a flock...."

This heavenly Shepherd *carries* his injured and exhausted sheep. He *leads* them faithfully to green pastures and quiet streams. He *cares* for the weakest with the same commitment he extends to the strongest. No wonder the image of God as Shepherd runs throughout the Old Testament!

Toward the end of Ecclesiastes—a bracing literary work most noted for its author's persistent cry of "Meaningless! Meaningless! Everything is meaningless!"—the cynical writer nonetheless cannot keep himself from recalling at least a fleeting image of God as Israel's Shepherd: "The words of the wise are like goads, their collected sayings like firmly embedded nails—given by one Shepherd" (Ecclesiastes 12:11). Why "Shepherd"? Why not, "given by one Carpenter"? It would seem to make more literary sense. But no. It is the image of God as Shepherd that darts into the mind of this ancient Israelite, even if he had chosen throughout his life to wander from the flock.

In a text with strong messianic overtones, the prophet Isaiah gives us one of the most touching and tender portraits of God as Shepherd to be found in the Bible. Although he tells us that "the Sovereign LORD comes with power, and his arm rules for him," he adds that this very God "tends his flock like a shepherd: He gathers the lambs in his arms and carries them close to his heart; he gently leads those that have young" (Isaiah 40:10–11).

A passage like this reveals how deeply the English language can sometimes let us down. We have a word for "allpowerful," namely "omnipotent." But where is our word for all-loving? Yet that is the word required here. Yes, Isaiah says, the omnipotent God is coming to earth to rule, and no one may frustrate even the tiniest portion of his will. Yet this same God also comes with infinite love, a tender affection like that of a caring shepherd who cradles his lambs next to his breast and leads his helpless ewes with understanding and boundless compassion.

Even the prophet Jeremiah, who had so much to say about bad shepherds (as we saw in chapter 2), could not stand to focus exclusively on the negative. In fact, he fairly bursts to speak of the kind of Shepherd who embodies everything good. Inspired by the Holy Spirit, the prophet conveys these words from the mouth of the Shepherd of Israel:

> I myself will gather the remnant of my flock out of all the countries where I have driven them and will bring them

back to their pasture, where they will be fruitful and increase in number. I will place shepherds over them who will tend them, and they will no longer be afraid or terrified, nor will any be missing. (Jeremiah 23:3–4)

In case anyone missed his point, Jeremiah repeats the message in Jeremiah 31:10: "He who scattered Israel will gather them and will watch over his flock like a shepherd."

Ezekiel, Jeremiah's young protégé, picks up on this theme in chapter 34 of his own book. He writes:

> For this is what the Sovereign LORD says: I myself will search for my sheep and look after them. As a shepherd looks after his scattered flock when he is with them, so will I look after my sheep. I will rescue them from all the places where they were scattered on a day of clouds and darkness. I will bring them out from the nations and gather them from the countries, and I will bring them into their own land. I will pasture them on the mountains of Israel, in the ravines and in all the settlements in the land. I will tend them in a good pasture, and the mountain heights of Israel will be their grazing land. There they will lie down in good grazing land, and there they will feed in a rich pasture on the mountains of Israel. I myself will tend my sheep and have them lie down, declares the Sovereign LORD. I will search for the lost and bring back the strays. I will bind up the injured and strengthen the weak, but the sleek and the strong I will destroy. I will shepherd the flock with justice. (Ezekiel 34:11–16)

What a picture! God seeks out the sheep scattered under evil shepherds; he looks after them; he rescues them; he gathers them; he pastures them; he feeds them; he tends them; he has them lie down; he searches for the lost; he brings back the strays; he binds up the injured; he strengthens the weak—and he does not leave the guilty unpunished! Those who grew fat on the misery of their fellow sheep are to be destroyed. Such is the absolute justice of the Shepherd God.

Can we learn anything from this metaphor, anything to guide us in our own work as undershepherds? Do I really have to ask?

God goes out of his way to use the image of a shepherd to describe his relationship with his people. But why? Why does he use that model in preference to others? It's not simply that Israel had shepherds. Israelites busied themselves in many occupations: carpenters, military officers, farmers, merchants, potters, kings, and the like. In addition, shepherds were considered the lowlifes of Israel! So why did God choose *that* metaphor to describe himself?

I think the reason can be found in its utter distinctiveness. The shepherd model features elements to be found nowhere else. What comes to mind when you think of a king? Power. What image floods your brain when you hear the word "merchant"? Money. What picture takes shape when you consider a farmer? Hard toil. But what do you think of when you call to mind a shepherd? Tender care. Faithful leadership. Strength. Courage. Determination. Personal attention.

As commentator William Barclay reminds us, "The word shepherd should paint a picture to us of the unceasing vigilance and patience of the love of God; and it should remind us of our duty towards our fellow-men, especially if we hold any kind of office in the Church of Christ."[3]

JESUS AS SHEPHERD

Since Jesus Christ is "the radiance of God's glory and the exact representation of his being," since he is "in very nature God" and "the image of God," and since Jesus himself declared, "Anyone who has seen me has seen the Father"—is it any surprise that the New Testament identifies Jesus as the Good Shepherd?[4]

This delightful identification goes far back into history, before Jesus' earthly life, even before his birth, back to the seventh or eighth century B.C. and the prophetic ministry of the little-known prophet Micah. About the same time that the great prophet Isaiah was peering into the future and writing of the coming Messiah, Micah was moved by God to predict the birthplace and a little of the ministry of the future Anointed One. His famous prophecy in Micah 5:2 declares, "But you, Bethlehem Ephrathah, though you are small among the clans of Judah, out of you will come for me one who will be ruler over Israel, whose origins are from of old, from ancient times."

That's where most of us stop reading, content to know the predicted place of the Messiah's birth. That is unfortunate, because just a few verses beyond this familiar passage lies another that describes how this Messiah will spend his time:

> He will stand and shepherd his flock
>   in the strength of the LORD.
>   in the majesty of the name of the LORD his God.
> And they will live securely, for then his greatness
>   will reach to the ends of the earth.
> And he will be their peace. (Micah 5:4–5)

When Matthew composed his Gospel centuries later, apparently he wished not only to emphasize Jesus' birthplace but also his ministry, for the Evangelist conflated these two texts into one neatly summarized prophecy: "But you, Bethlehem, in the land of Judah, are by no means least among the rulers of Judah; for out of you will come a ruler who will be the shepherd of my people Israel" (Matthew 2:6). In Matthew's opinion, Jesus' role as Shepherd took on such great importance that he felt compelled to give it some of the spotlight normally reserved for Bethlehem!

Near the end of his Gospel, as at its beginning, Matthew emphasizes the shepherding aspects of Jesus' ministry. In Matthew 25:32 he pictures the Savior dividing his sheep like a shepherd, while in Matthew 26:31 he quotes Zechariah

13:7 to remind his readers that Jesus also suffered for the sake of his sheep.

Without dispute, however, the greatest of all New Testament passages about Jesus the Shepherd is found in John 10. William Barclay accurately notes, "There is no better loved picture of Jesus than the Good Shepherd. The picture of the shepherd is woven into the language and imagery of the Bible."[5] Especially in John 10! Who can forget the marvelous claims Jesus makes for himself in this cherished chapter of the Bible? Savor just a few of them once again:

- "I am the gate for the sheep ... whoever enters through me will be saved." (verses 7, 9)
- "I am the good shepherd." (verse 11)
- "I know my sheep and my sheep know me." (verse 14)
- "I lay down my life for the sheep." (verse 15)
- "I have other sheep that are not of this sheep pen. I must bring them also." (verse 16)
- "They too will listen to my voice, and there shall be one flock and one shepherd." (verse 16)
- "You do not believe because you are not my sheep." (verse 26)
- "My sheep listen to my voice; I know them, and they follow me." (verse 27)
- "I give them eternal life, and they shall never perish." (verse 28)
- "No one can snatch them out of my hand." (verse 29)

No wonder millions of Christians through the ages have counted this chapter as their favorite. The portrait of Jesus painted here conveys all the warmth, security, strength, hope, and intimacy for which every human heart longs.

This portrait takes on even more significance once a reader gains an appreciation for the realities of Judean shepherding. Judea was not an easy place to live. The rough, stony ground of the countryside lent itself better to pastoral pursuits than to agricultural ones. Therefore,

> the most familiar figure of the Judaean uplands was the shepherd. His life was very hard. No flock ever grazed without a shepherd, and he was never off duty. There being little grass, the sheep were bound to wander, and since there were no protecting walls, the sheep had constantly to be watched. On either side of the narrow plateau the ground dipped sharply down to the craggy deserts, and the sheep were always liable to stray away and get lost. The shepherd's task was not only constant but dangerous, for, in addition, he had to guard the flock against wild animals, especially against wolves, and there were always thieves and robbers ready to steal the sheep.[6]

And what of the shepherd himself? He would appear

> sleepless, farsighted, weather-beaten, leaning on his staff and looking out over his scattered sheep, every one of them on his heart. You understand why the shepherd of Judaea sprang to the front of his people's history, why they gave his name to their king and made him the symbol of providence. Why Christ took him as the type of self-sacrifice. Constant vigilance, fearless courage, patient love for his flock, were the necessary characteristics of the shepherd.[7]

All along the way, a picture of intimacy bubbles to the surface. To highlight this, Barclay contrasts the way sheep were raised in Palestine and in Great Britain. British sheep were raised for food, fattened up, and killed so the farmer could move on to the next one. Palestinian sheep, on the other hand, were raised primarily for production of wool, so the relationship between shepherd and sheep remained long-term.

I wonder: Are the sheep in our churches of Palestinian or British stock? And what would they say if we asked *them*?

A friend of mine owns several sheep. Actually, it would be better to say that his wife owns them. When they moved not too long ago, my friend tried to get those sheep onto the back of a truck—they wouldn't budge. They locked their heels. They bleated. They pulled away from him. They simply would not allow him to move them.

But when his wife came out and spoke their names (Ramsey and Eunice), immediately they followed her right onto the truck. Why? Because she was the one who cared for them, who fed them, who healed them, who loved them. They knew her voice, and they trusted her voice. It was the voice of their shepherd.

That is exactly the picture Jesus painted of his intimate relationship with his sheep. Jesus knows his sheep, they know his voice, and they rest in his love for them, a love so extreme it led him to lay down his life for them. That is the Good Shepherd, and he's our preeminent model.

Jesus' self-portrait left such a deep imprint on his disciples' consciousness that the New Testament church could never get away from it. The writer of Hebrews begins to wind up his magnificent book with a reference to "our Lord Jesus, that great Shepherd of the sheep" (Hebrews 13:20). The apostle Peter, decades after his beachside conversation with his Lord, where Jesus charged him to "Feed my lambs.... Take care of my sheep.... Feed my sheep" (John 21:15, 16, 17), calls the Savior "the Shepherd and Overseer of your souls" and "the Chief Shepherd" (1 Peter 2:25; 5:4).

How appropriate, then, that in the final book of the Bible, as in the first, the divine Shepherd makes his presence felt. In Revelation 7 an angel describes to the apostle John the blessed fate awaiting uncounted martyrs who stand before the throne of God:

> He who sits on the throne will spread his tent over them.
> Never again will they hunger;
>   never again will they thirst.

The sun will not beat upon them,
  nor any scorching heat.
For the Lamb at the center of the throne will be their shep-
    herd;
  he will lead them to springs of living water.
And God will wipe away every tear from their eyes.
    (Revelation 7:15–17)

Who wouldn't follow such a Shepherd? What church wouldn't grow under the care of such a strong and tender pastor?

So why don't we strive to follow his lead more than we do?

HUMAN LEADERS AS SHEPHERDS

Many of the leaders God chose to guide his people, especially in the Old Testament, spent several years training for their future roles by caring for flocks of sheep. Consider Moses. This greatest of Jewish leaders learned some of his finest lessons in the desert of Midian, chasing the sheep of his father-in-law (see Exodus 3:1). Apparently God thought that the shepherd's life would well prepare a man to lead his people. A delightful Jewish legend explains why God chose Moses:

> When Moses was feeding the sheep of his father-in-law
> in the wilderness, a young kid ran away. Moses followed
> it until it reached a ravine, where it found a well to drink
> from. When Moses got up to it he said: "I did not know
> that you ran away because you were thirsty. Now you
> must be weary." He took the kid on his shoulders and
> carried it back. Then God said, "Because you have shown
> pity in leading back one of a flock belonging to a man,
> you shall lead my flock Israel."[8]

There's no telling if the legend has any basis in fact, but at least one indisputable fact can be confirmed in Isaiah 63:11, namely, that God, through the prophet, called Moses "the shepherd of his flock."

And shepherd to the end he was. As the great man prepared to step out of the pages of history and into eternity, he made one last request of the Lord. "May the LORD, the God of the spirits of all mankind, appoint a man over this community to go out and come in before them, one who will lead them out and bring them in, so the LORD's people will not be like sheep without a shepherd" (Numbers 27:16–17). The Lord granted Moses' request, and Joshua became not only the second leader of liberated Israel but its second shepherd as well.

If Moses was Israel's greatest leader, then David was its greatest king. He, perhaps more than any other human figure in the Old Testament, earned the label "shepherd." Like Moses, he trained for his national leadership responsibilities as a shepherd. When the proper time had arrived, the Lord told him, "You will shepherd my people Israel, and you will become their ruler" (2 Samuel 5:2). Years later, when Asaph reflected on David's rule, he wrote:

> [The LORD] chose David his servant
>   and took him from the sheep pens;
> from tending the sheep he brought him
>   to be the shepherd of his people Jacob,
>   of Israel his inheritance.
> And David shepherded them with integrity of heart;
>   with skillful hands he led them. (Psalm 78:70–72)

So great an impression did this shepherd-king make on his people that centuries later the prophet Ezekiel resurrected his memory with a startling prediction: "I will place over them one shepherd, my servant David, and he will tend them; he will tend them and be their shepherd" (Ezekiel 34:23; see also 37:24). While interpreters vary in their understanding of this prophecy—some say the prophecy refers to Christ, "the Son of David," while others contend that the literal David will be resurrected to take the place appointed for him—the correct interpretation matters little for our purposes. The main point is that David became known as a great leader precisely because he made a terrific shepherd. Hundreds of years after his death, David was not remembered as much for his amazing military exploits or his political reforms as for his ability to shepherd his people with integrity of heart.

What made David such an effective leader and a successful shepherd? A big part of it must have been the time he spent alone with his sheep, time he could use to meditate on his relationship with God. As a young man, David had plenty of time alone, time to meet with God and get to know him. Although he had twenty-four-hour-a-day responsibilities, he didn't have twenty-four-hour-a-day activity. At times the sheep would grow still and quiet; that's when a wise shepherd gets to know his God. That's the time for reflection and study and prayer. (Our Lord was never a shepherd in vocation, but he continually practiced this discipline of getting away to commune with God. The Good Shepherd didn't desert his sheep, but he made sure he didn't run down in the midst of the sheep.)

I imagine a lot was going on those nights when David watched over the sleeping flock. After caring for his sheep in the fields all day, he knew their needs. He didn't need to guess how he could best minister to the flock. And I suppose that some nights he looked up at the stars and wondered aloud to God, "What is man, that you are mindful of him?" He thought about God, but in a way rooted in his day-to-day life. Good theology doesn't drift in never-never land. It is rooted in the problems and difficulties of real life. I cannot help but wonder: How many pastors are missing that? I doubt that the current leadership model has helped pastors much in this regard.

I also wonder how much of David's theological reflection in the Psalms comes out of his shepherd lifestyle and mind-set. Most of it? Do the Psalms arise largely out of David's shepherding experience? It's obvious that we don't find the same kind of perspective in Solomon's writings. We find some interesting material there, but nothing like the depth we see in David. David contemplates the magnificence of God. Solomon, however, says things like, "Yeah, I ran off with these women, and here's what I learned: Fear God and keep the commandments. Adultery doesn't pay."

When you see yourself as a shepherd, I think you're much more likely to take a walk at night, to talk to God about his sheep, and to meditate on your own shepherding. You tend to ask God, "What are you trying to reveal of yourself in the midst of this?" God is a revelatory God. In the Bible he often says things like, "My sheep didn't understand this or that about me. I tried to show them, but they just didn't get it." However, David *the shepherd* did get much of it, probably because he spent time talking and listening to God during those quiet moments when the sheep were asleep.

And when David didn't get it—when he wandered away like an errant sheep—how did God grab the king's attention? By pricking his tender shepherd's heart. After David had committed adultery with Bathsheba and refused to repent for more than a year, the prophet Nathan told David a story about a wealthy man who had killed a poor family's only lamb just so he wouldn't have to sacrifice one of his own. David reacted with fury. "The man doesn't deserve to live!" he stormed. Moments later, however, David's vocal chords grew silent as Nathan replied, "You are the man!" Still, the dam had been broken. David was free at last to repent and to restore his relationship with God— and it all came about when Nathan brought the king back to his shepherd's roots (2 Samuel 12:1–13).

I simply cannot imagine the story in another setting. It simply doesn't work to have Nathan say, "You know, you have this down-line manager who's just not producing the teams necessary to capture the kingdom." Nathan broke David's heart by appealing to his shepherd's heart.

Compare this to Samuel's confrontation with King Saul. Even when the prophet told Saul that God would have given him the entire kingdom if he had obeyed, Saul refused to repent. He remained utterly unmoved by the royal imagery.

Now, quite frankly, David sinned more than Saul did. Saul spared some literal sheep when he should have killed them; David committed adultery with one human sheep and murdered another. Yet when Nathan used pastoral imagery in his story, David crumbled. Saul never did. Of course, Saul never tended sheep; he drove oxen and worked donkeys. He looked good, stood tall, and had a name the people could pronounce—but he never cared for a flock. And why would he? To him, they were just another herd to be driven.

David's story makes me ponder what God would have to say to me, a pastor, to force me to deal with the difficult issues of my life. What world would the "right" words come out of? What language would God have to use? While we're at it, if God wanted to break your heart or alter the direction of your life or ministry, what would he say? Could he get to you through some sheep? Or are there only oxen and donkeys in your life?

OBJECTIONS TO OVERCOME

I have thought a great deal about why we seem so hesitant to embrace the one model of ministry that God has so consistently championed throughout redemptive history, and I have concluded there may be several reasons behind our reticence.

1. We Fear Past Abuses That Went by the Name of "Shepherding."

In the "Shepherding Movement" that came out of Kansas City several decades ago, people were treated as if they really *were* sheep. "We'll make all the decisions for your life," these leaders said, "and you won't have to worry about a thing. We'll decide who you are to marry, where you are to live, and what kind of job you should hold."

This movement failed largely because it took a metaphor and attempted to turn it into a literal truth. Yes, the Bible sometimes calls us sheep, but that doesn't mean we are like sheep in every respect. We don't walk on four legs. We don't graze on hills or grow wool. Whenever I hear preachers say, "We're as dumb as sheep," I say to myself, "Well, thank you very much. I just feel blessed this morning."

When the Bible calls God's people sheep, it means that there are certain similarities, likenesses, and points of identification between us and sheep. But it is absurd to take the metaphor literally. Human "sheep" know that they're supposed to eat; they just need the shepherd to help them find the right kind of food. They know how to procreate, so there is little need for a shepherd to become involved. Whenever we take a metaphor too far, it becomes destructive. God never intended it to go as far as some have taken it.

So what *is* God trying to convey about his sheep? That they need a fold for their growth, development, and protection. That they need a shepherd to give them direction and care. That left to themselves, they are prone to wander and be scattered. And that's about it. To take the metaphor beyond the Bible's clearly intended meaning often leads to serious abuses. People don't want someone clubbing them over the head or fleecing them or grinding them up into shepherd's pie—at least, I know *I* don't.

So let me say this as plainly as I can: I am *not* advocating a return to the Shepherding Movement. What I *am* advocating is a return to the biblical idea of leader-as-shepherd, a person called by God to care for the Lord's flock. I believe it's not only what people are crying out for, but also what God has ordained from time immemorial.

2. We Are Repulsed by the Unsophisticated Nature of the Idea.

I think many Westerners reject the shepherd model because they consider it primitive, outdated, and unsophisticated. That was the problem of Lynn Anderson's friend quoted at the beginning of this chapter, and I suspect many others share his distaste for the idea.

Still, I hope you've begun to see that the traits of the shepherd as laid out in the Bible are exactly what people are looking for today. They want connectedness, relationships, security. They want to feel as if they matter, not as though they're simply a cog in an impersonal machine. They want to feel love, not merely hear it defined from the original Greek and Hebrew.

So to those of you who feel repulsed by the unsophisticated aura of the metaphor, I say: Try it, you'll like it. It's better than anything else out there!

3. Some Pastors Equate the Shepherd Model With Outdated Church Activities.

Pastors sometimes think the shepherd model would require them to have tea and coffee with everyone in the church at least once a year. I admit that some churches still have such a requirement in their constitutions; the pastor must visit every member family a minimum of once a year. So because pastors have struggled with such a system, they've left the shepherd model for the rancher model.

The main problem is that this produces a change of identity. One emphasizes caring; the other branding. The rancher sticks the cattle out on the range and leaves them to fend for themselves, then after a while rounds 'em up to see who's left. Not so the shepherd! He wants to spend time with his sheep. It's part of his nature.

Although we live by grace, it is a natural human tendency to reduce everything to a law. But that isn't how a shepherd lives. He doesn't say, "I have to rebuke this sheep twice and be with that sheep three times." He does whatever is needed at the time. His interactions with the sheep are individualized. There is no "law" for him except that he continue to be a shepherd.

Does the shepherd model mean that the pastor must go back to being the primary staff visitor to the congregation? Of course not. Ephesians 4 instructs us to equip the sheep for the work of ministry, and that includes visiting.

"Yes," someone will object, "but in my congregation of two thousand, if I spend time with even thirty members this year, the rest will be angry." Well, maybe. Jesus viewed himself as a shepherd and saw his people as sheep, yet he spent the majority of his time with three of the twelve disciples. He didn't spend equal time with the five thousand on the hill, but he never quit being the shepherd.

"That's tough if you're one of the five thousand," someone else might complain. To which I reply, "You've been reading my mail!" But as a shepherd, I have the primary responsibility to train, equip, and shepherd certain members (elders, staff members). As Joe Stowell writes:

> An effective shepherd understands that the substance of shepherding love goes beyond liking and chooses to focus on the needs of the flock. He understands that it is a matter of loving through a commitment that relates positively and constructively to the needs of those in his flock regardless of his own perspectives or pleasure. The shepherd checks his bag of resources to substantively meet real needs. He checks his time, talents, treasures, programs, alliances, and networks with other people and their resources. He checks the stockpile of the gifts of those in the extended flock and then seeks to marshal appropriate resources, whether they be his own or those of others, to focus like a laser beam of love on particular and personal needs within the assembly.[9]

Nevertheless, I also need to walk among the rest of the sheep. It can't always be with the elders and deacons and other leaders. As shepherd, I must be proactive in getting in touch with a broader base of my sheep.

People still think it's funny that my wife gets together with people who aren't on the Who's Who of the community. They say, "We saw your wife with the oddest group of people the other day." They mean that it wasn't the "in" group. I do similar things. There are other sheep I need to know besides leaders. I need to hear what's going on in the flock if I'm going to ensure that it is properly shepherded. One pastor told me that he has narrowed his church relationships to his staff and elders. I thought, *Man, talk about getting a distorted view!*

It's something like the king who put on pauper's clothing so he could walk around the kingdom unnoticed, enabling him to discover the reality of his people's living conditions. Susan and I went out to lunch after services one Sunday when we met a church couple whom we didn't know. They introduced themselves, and we sat down and ate with them. They had been wandering around the sheepfold and it was helpful to hear their hearts, their perspectives, what was happening in their lives. I think that must take place if we are to minister to all the members of the flock.

Unfortunately, some pastors isolate themselves from their people because they have adopted an inaccurate idea of their position. They think of themselves as prophets, for example, and therefore picture themselves on a hill, thundering down to the crowds below. They don't have a loving congregation as much as a trembling audience. That's not a New Testament way of thinking.

Although the Bible distinguishes between the sheep and their shepherd, it maintains a picture of the shepherd constantly walking among the flock. The shepherd is able to touch the individual faces of his sheep and know that they are his. The flock can hear his voice, and they know that he's their shepherd; he hasn't been off in his castle.

THE CALL TO BE SHEPHERDS

I believe that God is still calling the leaders of his people to become shepherds. Listen again to his ancient but ever-new commands:

- "Shepherd your people with your staff, the flock of your inheritance" (Micah 7:14).
- "Keep watch over yourselves and all the flock of which the Holy Spirit has made you overseers. Be shepherds of the church of God, which he bought with his own blood" (Acts 20:28).
- "Be shepherds of God's flock that is under your care, serving as overseers—not because you must, but because you are willing, as God wants you to be" (1 Peter 5:2).

Strive to be shepherds, God commands, not mere leaders. Be shepherds of the church of God, which he bought with his own blood. God says to us even today, "I spilled my blood for these men and women; they are my sheep. So shepherd them! Care for them! Love them!" And do so in the way he himself has modeled for us.

TIME FOR EVALUATION

How do you feel? After reading this chapter, are you saying, "Yes! That is what it's about. When God called me, I didn't know all the details, but I knew he had called me to something pretty special"? Or do you find yourself admitting, "You know, that's really not what I bought into when I took this job"?

Either way, I hope you have a better idea now of whether you're on the right track. If your spirit resonates with the biblical model of a pastor as shepherd, then no matter what difficulties you may be facing, you have more reason now to take heart than ever before. On the other hand, if you're thinking, "This isn't what I'd bargained for," then perhaps, just perhaps, you're not where God wants you to be.

What if you're not a pastor but a congregational leader? I hope you are also saying, "Yes! That's what church ought to be. That's what I've been looking for. So how do I help my pastor be that and release some of these other expectations? How can we free our pastor from one of these massive job descriptions formulated by humans?"

Whatever your situation, I hope the Scriptures we have looked at have provided some "Aha!" revelations for you—not all of which may have been pleasant. Frankly, I don't know how anyone can gaze at a picture of the shepherdhood of God and Christ and of our calling without saying, "Yes!" Once we are confronted with that picture, we must make a personal evaluation. Either we identify with it or we don't. Either we are called to it or we are not. Either we strive by God's Spirit to become increasingly like it—and if necessary, to repent and pursue it—or, for the flock's sake, we leave the pastorate.

I don't think this is harsh. Quite the contrary. Such a hard evaluation is simply what love demands. As Joe Stowell has written:

> Love is at the heart of what it means to be a shepherd. Shepherds are caring, flock-focused individuals whose primary motivation is not the interest of self but the interest of the safety, security, and satisfaction of the flock. Given this, a discussion of love in terms of the shepherd's ministry is of great importance. And it must be more than a discussion. It must lead to a commitment that transcends the circumstances of the shepherd's life or the configuration of the shepherd's congregation. True love does not *depend* on its environment; it dramatically *affects* its environment.[10]

What a stunning model God has given us of what it means to be a shepherd of the sheep! Dwell there; live there. God will bring great power to a church led by a caring shepherd, because God loves his shepherds.

Abel was a shepherd, and God received an excellent sacrifice through him. Jacob was a shepherd, and God showed his grace through Jacob. Job was a shepherd, and God showed him faithfulness in the midst of great suffering. David was a shepherd, and God brought his people to glory through David. Amos was a shepherd, and God spoke to a rebellious people through him. And Jesus is the Good Shepherd, God incarnate, who gave his life for the sheep.

The biblical model still makes sense. What's more, the model that God established in the Scriptures fits perfectly with surveys that tell us what people are looking for. I guess God really does know what he's talking about, after all!

Chapter 7

LEADER OR SHEPHERD?

O ne influential evangelical has recently looked at the decline of the American church and boldly declared that our problem is that "we have too many pastors and not enough leaders." Whatever he perceives pastors to be, he thinks they are the problem. And whatever he perceives leaders to be, he thinks they are the answer. Millions have accepted this analysis, and today we have no lack of leadership books, seminars, curricula, training aids, and the like ... but still the church struggles.

Can anyone doubt that the current pastoral model favored in the church is "leader"? Much good has been written and urged on pastors regarding their leadership of the church. I myself have read at least a hundred books on leadership and management.

But is "leader" really the model the Bible implores us to put at center stage? Would the church honestly be better off if we pastors thought of ourselves first as leaders and only secondarily as shepherds? You'd think so if current bestsellers were any accurate indication.

THE AMERICAN CHURCH ANALYZED

George Barna's *The Second Coming of the Church* is a good representative of this trend. In most ways this is an excellent, well-researched, and much-needed book. Barna clearly loves the church and wants it to become the culture-transforming power that God meant it to be. I have tremendous respect and admiration for him and am thankful for the positive impact that he has had. I love those who love the church.

Barna has studied the church thoroughly, and in *The Second Coming* he meticulously documents its weaknesses and shortcomings. He does this not as a doomsayer but as an instigator of change. As such, he makes comments such as:

> For several decades, the Church has relied upon greater sums of money, better techniques, bigger numbers and facilities, and more impressive credentials as the means to influence society at large. These elements have failed us; in our efforts to serve God, we have crowded out God Himself.[1]

> Rather than seeing the existing woes of the Church as a precursor to collapse, why not identify the reasons behind the mounting disappointment with the Church and strive to convert our understanding of and concern for people's unmet spiritual needs into a viable alternative? If we allow our visionary leaders to provide a biblically based, alternative Christian experience that empowers people to know, love, and serve God in authentic and vital ways, millions of purpose-starved Americans will respond.[2]

> In its new iteration, the Church must reinvent itself as a movement of believers zealously seeking to infect others with Christ's love and a passion to serve others.[3]

Barna begins and ends his book with the same stirring challenge. In the preface to his work he writes, "Some day God will ask you for an account of how you used the gifts and resources He entrusted to you for His purposes,"[4] while in the book's final chapter he reiterates, "It is not somebody else's responsibility to improve matters. Someday God will ask you to give an account for your time on earth. What report of your commitment to practical, holy, life-transforming service will you be able to give Him?"[5]

So what will enable the church to meet this challenge? Barna says we need "spiritual revolutionaries" who embody the traits of personal righteousness, sincerity, humility, trustworthiness, love, and perseverance.

Terrific stuff! I couldn't agree more. Barna even begins his eighth chapter as follows:

> Jesus must experience a sense of *déjà vu* as He surveys the American church today. It was just two millennia ago that He ministered among the people of Israel and felt His heart sink in sadness. "When he saw the crowds, he had compassion on them, because they were harassed and helpless, like sheep without a shepherd" (Matt. 9:36).
>
> This verse is a vivid image of the Church today: millions of people busily engaged in meaningless activity in a vain attempt to find purpose, direction, and comfort, but pitifully mired in chaos and confusion. It is neither the condition God intended for us, nor a necessary state of affairs.[6]

Since he had just quoted Matthew 9:36 and equated the church today with the "sheep" of Jesus' day, you might think that Barna would suggest "shepherds" as the cure for a sick flock. But you would be wrong. Even though he agrees that today's church can be likened to sheep without a shepherd, he thinks that effective leaders, not caring shepherds, are the solution.

A leader, Barna explains, "is someone who effectively motivates, mobilizes resources, and directs people toward the fulfillment of a jointly embraced vision."[7] And a *Christian* leader is "someone who is called by God to lead and possess virtuous character and effectively motivates,

mobilizes resources, and directs people toward the fulfillment of a jointly embraced vision from God."[8] Such a
leader, he says, must especially possess three special elements: "*calling* or anointing; godly *character*; and leadership
competencies."

As I said, there is much here to wildly applaud and
avidly support. But why does Barna christen leaders, rather
than shepherds, as the hope of the church? The reason
seems to be that he equates "shepherds" or "pastors" with
"teachers." A high percentage of the pastors he spoke with
in his research admitted they loved to teach but felt neither
called nor gifted to lead. One pastor told Barna, "I don't see
myself as a visionary, but as a shepherd. So focusing people
on a large-range view of where they're going is very hard
for me. Half the time, I'm not sure myself."[9] Because this
pastor and many others equated their teaching gifts with
their pastoral role, Barna simply followed suit. The result is
a book-wide misidentification of shepherd with teacher. No
wonder Barna opts instead for "leader"!

A little later in the book Barna contrasts leaders with
both teachers and managers, but he never returns to the
shepherd metaphor. Nowhere does he deal with Ephesians
4:11, which describes the "pastor-teacher." In Barna's
approach, a pastor *is* a teacher. Thus a false dichotomy
extends through the entire book.

In fact, the qualities Barna lists under "leaders" can just
as well be said to characterize good shepherds. Shepherds
ought to have vision and character because sheep won't
trust a shepherd with faulty character. What about direction
and motivation? A good shepherd must embody both. The
shepherd says to his sheep, "We're going over here because
that is where you'll find the water and grass and safety you
need."

"But Glenn," someone might ask, "if what you say is
true, does it really make much difference whether you call
such a person a leader or a shepherd? Aren't Barna and you

talking about the same person? Isn't this just a matter of semantics?"

Not really. The "shepherd" and "leader" metaphors convey quite different messages, especially when each is allowed to take center stage. While a shepherd must possess some qualities of leadership, a leader need not connect at all with the caring heart of a shepherd.

I rejoice when I read Barna's declaration that "ours is not the business of organized religion, corporate worship, or Bible teaching. . . . Those are fragments of a larger purpose to which we have been called by God. We are in the business of life transformation."[10] Amen! But I would also insist that, in the same way, "leadership" is merely a "fragment" of the larger purpose to which we have been called as shepherds. We are in the business of shepherding God's flock.

I love what Joe Stowell has written on this issue:

> Unfortunately, we often perceive ministry through management paradigms that place the pastor, if not at the top of the chart, second only to the board of elders, with those in the church falling below them in a scattered array of functions. While it is accurate to say that that shepherd *does* hold a particular sense of biblical authority in the flock, when it comes to function, the biblical organizational chart has the mission of the church at the top; under that, like a reverse pyramid, are the people in the flock; and beneath them, at the bottom point of the upside down pyramid, is the pastor, to serve all of those in the flock with enabling resources to help them become all they need to be in order to advance the mission of His church. This captures the mind-set of a servant shepherd. His heart lives in the what-can-I-do-to-help mode.[11]

Likewise, Jay Adams concludes that "the work to which the Christian minister is called therefore is essentially *pastoral*."[12]

THE MISSING METAPHORS

I think it is significant that, although the Bible tells pastors to lead their flocks, it does not address them by the title "leader." The New Testament tells believers to "remember your leaders" (Hebrews 13:7), to "obey your leaders" (Hebrews 13:17), and to "greet all your leaders" (Hebrews 13:24). It also calls Judas Barsabbas and Silas "leaders among the brothers" (Acts 15:22) and reports that Paul spoke "privately to those who seemed to be leaders" (Galatians 2:2), but it assiduously avoids addressing church officials by the title "leader." Why?

In *Metaphors of Ministry*, David Bennett notes that Jesus drew his illustrations from numerous objects, activities, and roles of everyday life. The Lord used at least thirty-five images to describe his followers. Yet there were some significant omissions. Jesus did *not* use a number of words for his people, even though the social roles these words described would have been familiar to Jesus' listeners.[13]

For example, Jesus did not use even one of the numerous words compounded from the Greek root *arch*, a term that conveys rule and a strong tone of authority. At least sixteen of these words occur elsewhere in the New Testament—patriarch, tetrarch, etc.—but not one is *ever* applied to the disciples of Jesus, with the exception of Paul's description of himself in 1 Corinthians 3:10 as "an expert builder" (*architekton*) who laid the foundation for others to build on.

So my question is this: If none of these leadership or authoritative or ruler titles are used to describe pastors in the New Testament, why are *we* using them? Why are we building a model of ministry around the concept of leader, when the Bible itself largely avoids it?

LEADER VERSUS SHEPHERD

Although the words *leader* and *shepherd* do partially overlap in meaning, the approaches they represent are not identical. So what are the essential differences between these two models? What difference does it make which model we choose to make central? What happens when "leadership" rather than "shepherdship" becomes the primary model for the pastor? One way to begin such an inquiry is to compare some key aspects of each model:

Leader	*Shepherd*
People as product, a means to an end	People as a priority
Engineer, building systems and structures	Encourager of the flock
Manager	Minister
Turns people into objects	Knows people and calls them by name
Seeks church growth	Seeks personal growth of people
Focuses on programs	Focuses on people
Guided by a business model built on psychological and sociological studies	Guided by a biblical model rooted in God's identity as the Good Shepherd
Seeks self-fulfillment and self-actualization	Seeks spiritual fullness and absolute dependency on God

A leader model can never produce the kind of church that will transform the culture around it. Only a shepherd model can do that. That is why God does not call us to be leaders but shepherds. If our *goal* is faithful shepherdship, the *result* will be effective leadership. All too often, however, we err by making the result our goal. The problem is not that we have too many pastors and not enough leaders, but that we have too many man-made leaders and not enough God-called shepherds.

Does that mean there's no place for strong leaders who are not shepherds? Of course not. God appointed Nehemiah, for example, to rebuild Jerusalem's walls and to put the nation back on a God-honoring track. But that was the extent of his calling. When Nehemiah completed his job, he disappeared from biblical history a much-honored hero. Yet leadership does not disappear. In fact, the New Testament gives a prominent and honored place to the gift of leadership.

Leaders (whether generals or public works directors) are concerned primarily about getting a certain job done. While they must treat people wisely in order to complete the task, their first priority is not the people but the task. This crucial difference between shepherds and leaders can be seen clearly in the reigns of David and Solomon.

No one questions that King David possessed remarkable leadership abilities, but even today he is known not as a great leader but as the shepherd-king. Within a few years after David's death the people he had led remembered him as such:

> He [God] chose David his servant
>   and took him from the sheep pens;
> from tending the sheep he brought him
>   to be the shepherd of his people Jacob,
>   of Israel his inheritance.
> And David shepherded them with integrity of heart;
>   with skillful hands he led them. (Psalm 78:70–72)

Even when David seriously erred, he thought like a shepherd. For example, 2 Samuel 24 reports that when David sinfully took a census of the fighting men of Israel, against good advice, God responded by sending a plague on Israel that killed seventy thousand Israelites. At the climax of the carnage David cried out to God, "I am the one who has sinned and done wrong. These are but sheep. What have they done? Let your hand fall upon me and my family" (verse 17).

Without question, David led his people, but far more than that, he *shepherded* them. And that's the biggest reason why the nation never lost its love for its revered shepherd-king.

Contrast that with Solomon, David's son. Solomon expanded the nation's borders like no king before or after him. He "made silver and gold as common in Jerusalem as stones" (2 Chronicles 1:15). He built a powerful cavalry, increased trade, and operated lucrative mines. He is the king who spent seven years building God's first temple in Jerusalem (and almost twice as long—thirteen years—erecting his own palace). Renowned for his wisdom and infamous for his political connections, Solomon exemplifies many of the traits coveted by strong leaders: vision galore, powerful motivational skills, a strategic planner par excellence. He was a man who got things done.

But no one ever called him "shepherd." In fact, by the end of his prosperous reign, the people under his care were tired, exhausted, and spent. "Your father put a heavy yoke on us," these haggard people told Solomon's son and successor, Rehoboam, "but now lighten the harsh labor and the heavy yoke he put on us, and we will serve you" (1 Kings 12:4). Can't you almost hear the bleats of a weary flock dying for a good rest in a green pasture by a quiet stream? But Rehoboam, like Solomon, didn't want to be a shepherd. In fact, he told these exhausted sheep that he'd be twice the "leader" his father was ... and the nation unraveled (1 Kings 12:19).

Now, I'm not saying that all leaders act as harshly as did Solomon or Rehoboam. But I am saying that a pastor who thinks of himself as "leader" more than as "shepherd" will tend to give priority to projects over people, chores over community. In the long run it's almost inevitable.

Consider what happens with stragglers. A leader isn't greatly concerned if one or two fall by the wayside. If they can't keep up, a leader reasons, they'll be better off in some other, slower-moving flock. A shepherd, on the other hand, refuses to leave sheep behind. When Jacob was driving his flocks to meet Esau, he said to his estranged brother:

> My lord knows that the children are tender and that I must care for the ewes and cows that are nursing their young. If they are driven hard just one day, all the animals will die. So let my lord go on ahead of his servant, while I move along slowly at the pace of the droves before me and that of the children, until I come to my lord in Seir. (Genesis 33:13–14)

Jacob, a true shepherd, expressed genuine concern for the weakest and the most vulnerable among his flock. Such concern is simply not built into the leader model.

So how fast is too fast? How slow is too slow? The robust sheep want to run ahead, but you can't abandon the weaker ones in the back. If you're a shepherd, you're always struggling with this tension. When the flock is exhausted, you can't drive them hard. You constantly have to say, "I want to bring this flock to health and wholeness and safety, but I don't want to destroy any of the young or injured sheep. My church might indeed grow faster if I set a more aggressive pace, but if I did so at our stage, I fear I would lose some precious sheep entrusted to me." It's a constant struggle.

In short, the difference between "shepherd" and "leader" is not merely semantic. It makes all the difference in the world if I've been persuaded by human reasoning to adopt a model based on psychological and sociological principles or directed by the call of God on my life to shepherd his sheep.

LEADERSHIP: NEEDED, BUT NOT CENTRAL

Good shepherds must be leaders, but leadership is not the whole package. Shepherds do lead their flocks to still waters. They do protect their sheep, and they do guide them to safe pastures. But leadership is not at the core of a shepherd's job description, and that's where I part company with much of the contemporary focus on leadership.

Whenever I take one of those "giftedness" tests, it always reveals me to be a mix of pastor-teacher and leader, so don't think I have a bias against leaders or leadership. I am thankful that God included the gift of leadership among the *charismata* he lavished on the church! But it seems to me that the leadership gift must always be directed by the shepherd's heart and mind. That is why Jesus told his followers, "The kings of the Gentiles lord it over them; and those who exercise authority over them call themselves Benefactors. But you are not to be like that. Instead, the greatest among you should be like the youngest, and the one who rules like the one who serves" (Luke 22:25–26). Shepherds instinctively serve out of humility; leaders do not.

Still, I am a leader, and leadership is good and right and necessary and vital in its place. *But its place is not at the center.* Trouble always follows when leadership becomes central. Things may progress nicely for a while, as in Solomon's day, when gold and silver became as common as stones, but the long-term outlook is never good. When we make leadership the goal, the end result, people often feel used.

We also intimidate pastors who lack the leadership gift or who do not have it in great measure. If a pastor does not have the gift of leadership and is not secure in his identity as a shepherd, he will be intimidated by those with leadership or administrative gifts—and that intimidation will keep him from mobilizing the very people he needs to help lead the church in positive directions.

DO SHEPHERDS HAVE VISION?

Vision is a wonderful and necessary component of good leadership, but I'm concerned that too many people are following a leader's vision to their great detriment. A pastor I know who took over for a leader type still receives notes from his congregation like this: "You know, Pastor, we're beginning to know that you love us. We're beginning to see your shepherd's heart. But once burned, twice shy. Just give us time. We haven't had a shepherd before."

The leader whom this pastor replaced was a good man, a successful evangelist. He used his strong personality to urge the church to get people into the kingdom. Everyone was mobilized for that purpose—and along the way, a lot of sheep started bleeding. But when you're trying to quickly increase the size of the flock, there's really no time to stop and bind up the wounded.

There is a place for painting a vision for the church, but even vision isn't central. At Calvary I have preached regarding where I believe the church needs to go, but that vision will start to become a reality only when the members of the flock learn to trust me and my commitment to them. Otherwise, many will sit back and say, "Why should I follow you? You're just doing this to sell books or to get on *The 700 Club* or to be listed as the pastor of one of the ten most aggressive churches in the nation." But if my sheep know me and trust me, they will eventually see I have painted this vision for them to provide for them and to lead them to green pastures and cool, still waters.

A shepherd's vision for his church must always be tempered by his knowledge of the sheep and guided by their trust in him. This provides a safeguard against the danger of self-aggrandizement, the kind of mentality that says, "Look what I've done and where I want to go."

In the leadership model, the goal is to mobilize and move people to our vision. But the first thing pastors need to do is to spend time letting our people see our shepherd's heart, allowing them to get to know us and see us in action among them. My first responsibility as pastor is to build my credibility as a faithful shepherd, not to convince people to buy into my vision for the church. The shepherd builds a relationship of trust with the flock so that the sheep will follow to green pastures. The shepherd knows that his sheep cannot be what they are called to be for God, nor can they produce what God has called them to produce, unless he faithfully takes them where they need to go. And they will not go with him unless they know his voice. They must trust him.

A leader's effectiveness is built on vision, not trust or character. Shepherding is just the opposite. Shepherding is built on character, with vision growing out of earned trust. That means *the number one goal for a pastor is not to articulate a great vision but to help his sheep trust him and know him.*

Do you know why the military never uses drill sergeants to lead troops into battle? Because drill sergeants don't care about the soldiers. Their only job is to give recruits a vision of what a real soldier is all about. They teach you the basic skills, whip you into shape, and tell you what you should and shouldn't do. But in combat, the military shifts to a more relational model of leadership so that when a captain says, "This is for God and country!" you are ready to follow him up any hill.

I wonder: If I came to a new church and showed the people that I was a shepherd, that I cared for them—but did not yet have a vision for them—where would that congregation be in a year? Worst case? I might I be pastoring a church of forty or fifty people because my abilities and gifts wouldn't carry me beyond that. But is that so wrong? If those people are being effectively shepherded and seeing others come to Christ, is that bad? In reality, that describes 85 percent of our churches. I often speak to rural pastors who admit that their churches are growing only 1 to 2 percent a year while their towns continue to shrink. Doesn't that little church deserve a shepherd who models Christ?

On the other hand, where would that church be if I came as a leader with great vision but no shepherd's heart? I think the latter scenario could be much more destructive than the former. When I stand and thunder from the pulpit about my vision, I become Moses to that congregation. Soon they'll want a veil between us. "You go up the mountain," they'll say, "while we stay back here." And so the distance between us grows. I might eventually get them to the place of my vision, but they'll feel as if they're camping outside the restricted boundaries of my holy mount.

Why have we locked onto a grandiose vision of world conquest when God may simply be saying to us, "Here is this flock. It may never be large. It may never be influential. But be an effective and faithful shepherd with the group I've given you"?

Don't misunderstand. I have difficulty with a pastor in our culture who hasn't seen someone come to Christ in three years. I have friends ministering in the Muslim world where that's the norm, but it certainly is not common here. The shepherd model doesn't mean evangelism is a low priority. I am not suggesting that if you pastor in a little town, it's fine to shepherd your own people and not worry about anyone else coming to Christ.

Years ago I attended a pastor's conference in which a denominational leader gave some alarming statistics. "Some of your churches haven't baptized anybody or seen anybody come to faith in several years," he declared. One pastor stood up and replied, "Well, you have to understand, we've been spending these last three years building relationships." I couldn't help it. I blurted out, "My goodness, man, what kind of relationships have you been building?"

I knew the town in which this individual pastored. It wasn't a bastion of liberalism or a haven for skeptics or a stronghold of other religions. In fact, a church just three blocks away from his was exploding with people coming to Christ. But he hadn't seen anyone come to Christ in three years? I couldn't help thinking, *What a rationalization!*

Obviously, I don't endorse such an extreme. A real shepherd will get uneasy if his sheep aren't birthing lambs. A flock without some babies isn't healthy; someone has been neutered or spayed or something. True shepherds are not content to merely oversee the flock. They also want to see their flocks grow and thrive.

MODELS LEFT TO THEMSELVES

If both the leader and shepherd models are left to themselves, how do they tend to deteriorate? What happens in a worst-case scenario?

The leader model, left to itself, always tends toward abuse of power. Why? It seems to me that the leader model has its origins and rationale in history, in the experiences and examples given to us by great "leaders" of the past, many of whom accomplished a great deal but who sacrificed followers in the process.

The shepherd model, on the other hand, finds its origins in God. It intrigues me that, so far as I know, God doesn't call himself a leader anywhere in the Bible. Just substitute the word "leader" wherever "shepherd" appears in Psalm 23—it will curl your hair. It sounds absurd. It just doesn't feel right. "The Lord is my leader; I had better keep up. He drives me to green pastures...." And it gets downright scary if you use the German word for leader: "The Lord is my Führer...."

Given its historical origins, it's easy to see why the leader model tends toward abuse of power. How, then, does the shepherd model deteriorate? Back to lowliness, humility, and constant toil. The deterioration is much more benign. Even if I'm not the most gifted shepherd in the world, I can still care for a flock.

Of course, no one wants either bad leaders or bad shepherds. But I think bad leaders can (and do) cause much more mischief than bad shepherds. Granted, not all leaders are ironhanded, but the leader model much more readily slips into ironhandedness than does the shepherd model. It is far easier to think of an ironhanded leader than an ironhanded shepherd.

When a shepherd starts abusing power, it is clearly a violation of what it means to be a shepherd. But when a leader starts violating his power, it's not nearly so clear.

There is nothing built into the leader model to keep it from drifting into abuse of power. Where is the governor? Where is the standard by which we measure it? The standards are those of the leadership gurus, not the unchanging Word of God.

I believe this problem is reflected even in our recent presidential crisis. Despite his moral failures, Mr. Clinton insisted, "I can still be an effective leader." Maybe he could. But if he were a shepherd, could he have said, "I can still be an effective shepherd"? I doubt it. Sheep do not want to be lied to. They may be dumb, but they are not stupid. They know that the character of their shepherd does matter.

WHAT ABOUT A SERVANT-LEADER?

I think most people intuitively understand that the leader model can easily deteriorate into a grab for power, which explains why the term "servant-leader" has come into vogue. We realize that if we don't temper the idea of leader with the qualifying idea of servant, the leader model will usually degenerate into something we don't want. It's a natural progression, so we try to buffer the leader model with the word "servant"—yet all the concepts around which the leader model is built push against such a tempering.

I believe our discussions concerning servant-leadership arise from an outcry of a church sick and tired of leaders. God never says, "Here is your scepter," even if it comes wrapped in a towel. God says, "Here's a staff." The scepter may look rich, fancy, and impressive, but the Lord calls us to walk with a staff. We are not royalty, but shepherds toiling under the authority of the Great Shepherd.

I have heard speakers claim that when Jesus knelt down to wash his disciple's feet, he was demonstrating servant-leadership. I disagree. Jesus was not demonstrating servant-leadership at all but how the Good Shepherd takes care of dysfunctional sheep. How do you deal with sheep who just don't "get it"? You serve their needs. Why? Because you're their shepherd, not their leader. There's something powerful about that.

WHERE THE RUBBER MEETS THE ROAD

Recently in a sermon I told about the death of my friend Diane Ginter. Diane was my personal "prayer warrior," a devoted friend who petitioned God on my family's behalf more often than I will ever know.

Diane lived simply but had an incredible impact on the kingdom of God. I first met Diane after I had prayed that God would provide for me a Daniel Nash, the famed prayer intercessor for evangelist Charles Finney. Nash habitually traveled to a Finney crusade site weeks in advance, locked himself in a room, and prayed. If Finney was preaching and felt little response, he interrupted himself, found Nash, and asked him to pray harder and to intercede through the barriers. History records that when Nash died, Finney's revival ministry also came to a halt. His itinerant ministry ended.

One Saturday after Diane's death, I woke up in the middle of the night with the scary realization that my "Nash" had just died. "Is this it?" I asked. God pushed that question out of my mind but left me with the conviction that I simply had to proclaim Diane's story. I told my flock that many people had discounted this unassuming woman because she walked to a different drummer. Yet she had such an impact on my life! When a crisis once overwhelmed our family, Diane prayed and fasted several weeks on our behalf. She spent countless hours in intercessory prayer for us. As I talked about Diane and her ministry, I must confess that I got a little choked up. She meant that much to me.

In response, I received scores of letters from my sheep, all saying, "Pastor, thank you for being transparent." One of my staff members approached me with tears and said, "I saw your heart. I've never seen anything like that before."

All of a sudden it dawned on me that my church wanted a shepherd who cared about the sheep, who hurt for the sheep, who rejoiced with the sheep, who laughed with the sheep. But they wouldn't get that from the leader model with its in-control persona who knows exactly where everyone needs to be going.

One of my pastors has told me, "This is the first time in my life I haven't been judged on the numbers." I have held him accountable for numbers, but he doesn't feel judged on them. We both know the numbers are the result of something else. I ask him what he is doing, what ministry is happening, and what his "people orientation" is. The numbers may show something is wrong, but they're not the whole story.

As a shepherd who is also a leader, I have brought in business consultants to work with my staff in cross-functional relationships. We brainstormed and ministered to each other and came up with some useful ideas. The church's whole strategic plan fits on six pages. That's it. Any more complicated than that and I won't read it.

The main issue for me is building relationships. I use tools out of the leadership model to help us fulfill our pastoral responsibilities, but as I said to my team, "We need some structure, but we're first a community." We use leadership tools, but we use them out of a shepherd's grid. Leaders know how to run programs, but I want to change people's lives. That's why I'm so committed to the shepherd model.

GIVE 'EM WHAT THEY WANT

Because the church has floundered badly in the past few decades, we have adopted an executive CEO (leader) mindset that actually works against the needs of people and what they're looking for. Men and women are not really looking for leadership; they're looking for relationships. They say, "We want a pastor with integrity. We want someone who cares more about us than about building a big church. We want to feel loved. We want to be someplace where we belong. We don't want to feel used—we get that at work—and we *don't* want that here."

We need a generation of pastor-shepherds with a sharp vision, a clear sense of call, and a deep understanding of and a passionate love for people. We need shepherds willing to lie down in the doorway of the sheepfold, ready to give their lives for the sheep. Finally, we need shepherds who are truly thankful to God for allowing them the privilege of pastoring his sheep.

God has not called us to be merely the leaders of his church. We are not the CEOs of his church. We are not the ranchers of his church. We are not the administrators or managers or executives of his church.

So who are we? We are pastors, shepherds called by God, ordained by God, anointed by God, and placed over a flock by Almighty God. And we are to serve under him and him alone. If you are a pastor, God does not call you to be a leader but to be a shepherd of the sheep.

The men and women in our churches are sick and tired of leaders. They've heard too many false promises from the leaders of this world. They want faithful shepherds—and they will follow such a shepherd with joyful, passionate abandon.

Chapter 8

THE CALL OF GOD

A good friend of mine who used to teach at a well-known evangelical seminary once asked several of his classes, "Can you identify a sense of call to ministry?" Most of his students met the question with blank stares; they had no idea what their professor was talking about. Only about 30 percent in his most "enlightened" class could answer this question in the affirmative, while a scant 4 percent in his most uninformed class could say "yes."

My friend asked the same question of men and women headed to the mission field and into full-time evangelism—and found the same disturbing lack of call. When he asked one student, "Why are you attending seminary?" the young man replied, "So I can enter into a respectable, calm, professional ministry to provide for my family."

I gulped when I heard that. Could it be that such a rampant disregard of God's call to shepherd his flock is behind much of the decline we see in the American church? If pastoring is just another job, I can think of better things to do.

This disregard probably shouldn't surprise us. As I prepared to write this chapter, I scoured dozens of books that mentioned God's call, but almost all of them immediately dropped the topic to launch into discussions of preaching, managing, counseling, visiting, and the like. In essence, most of them said, "Make sure you're called, and then counsel, preach, visit, manage, and so forth." They don't all agree about what a call is, but they all say there ought to be one. Strangely, however, most never address the key piece.

Yet it's this sense of call that, like nothing else, is meant to fill us with a passionate sense of direction and destiny. Would a sovereign God leave us to our own devices to wander around hoping against hope that, just perhaps, we really might be suited for the pastorate?

I don't believe so. I agree with C. E. Colton, who wrote almost half a century ago:

> Every genuine preacher must feel the hand of God laid upon him for this specific task; otherwise his ministry will be unhappy and unproductive. Only the consciousness of a divine call to do a great and awful work can give that confidence and feeling of authority necessary to make one's ministry successful.[1]

WHAT IS A CALL?

One reason that "the call of God" has not received the attention it merits may be that the concept is not easy to pin down and define objectively. When we consider the Bible's most famous calls to ministry, we find that nearly all involved a physical, audible call, the actual voice of God summoning a person into his service.

It was this way with Moses: "The angel of the LORD appeared to him in flames of fire from within a bush.... When the LORD saw that he had gone over to look, God called to him from within the bush, 'Moses! Moses!... I am sending you to Pharaoh to bring my people the Israelites out of Egypt'" (Exodus 3:2, 4, 10).

So it was with Samuel: "The lamp of God had not yet gone out, and Samuel was lying down in the temple of the LORD, where the ark of God was. Then the LORD called Samuel. . . . Again the LORD called, 'Samuel!' . . . The LORD called Samuel a third time. . . . The LORD came and stood there, calling as at the other times, 'Samuel! Samuel!'" (1 Samuel 3:3–4, 6, 8, 10).

It was also this way with Paul:

> As he neared Damascus on his journey, suddenly a light from heaven flashed around him. He fell to the ground and heard a voice say to him, "Saul, Saul, why do you persecute me?"
>
> "Who are you, Lord?" Saul asked.
>
> "I am Jesus, whom you are persecuting," he replied. "Now get up and go into the city, and you will be told what you must do." (Acts 9:3–6)

But was it that way with me? No. In fact, few of us who believe God has called us into the pastorate can say the call was audible. Yet we continue to insist that the call was (and is) real. We applaud those who make comments such as this:

> Why would a person enter the ministry without a call? Yet it is felt by some that a call is unnecessary. . . . In such cases aptitude tests may be used to determine a person's vocational ability. Then, counselors recommend certain educational pursuits to develop the *natural* acumen. While some are more suited for sciences, others are channeled to social or humanitarian pursuits, one of which might be an involvement in the religious field. Of course, the born-again believer understands that although natural intelligence and aptitudes are not to be scorned or considered unimportant, these are not the final criteria in determining one's call to the ministry.[2]

I know of pastors who wonder, *Am I really called to this?* Many doubt their calling because they merely ambled through some menu of career options and said, "I don't want to be a lawyer, I don't want to be a mechanic, I don't want to be a psychologist. Maybe I'll be a pastor." Or even worse, someone gave them an aptitude test and told them, "You have all the qualities for the ministry."

We need to hear more about what it means to be called of God. One person described it as "FIF disease," that *Funny Interior Feeling* disease. This disease doesn't come from eating cold pizza, nor does it come from the prolonged study of Hebrew grammar. In fact, many pastors regard FIF disease as the beginning point of their ministry. They talk about a particular moment when they received a divine call they could not ignore.

John Wesley talked about his heart being strangely warmed. Francis of Assisi said he heard the voice of Christ while in chapel prayer. Jack Hayford, pastor of the Church on the Way in Van Nuys, California, wrote, "Three years ago, I invited pastors across the nation to write to me and describe as well as they could, 'The reason I'm in the ministry.' Unsurprisingly, yet a very telling fact, almost to the person the answer was the same: 'I was called by God.'"[3]

God will not be denied his sovereign right to choose the vessels he will use. What God stated about Saul of Tarsus—"This man is my chosen instrument" (Acts 9:15)—he also declares of others today.

WHAT DOES SCRIPTURE SAY?

Still, as we noted, it's not a cut-and-dried matter to define and describe what such a calling to vocational ministry looks like. While the Bible talks a great deal about God's call, most of these passages speak of how believers are "called to belong to Jesus Christ" (Romans 1:6), "called to be holy" (1 Corinthians 1:2), "called to one hope" (Ephesians 4:4), or "called to peace" (Colossians 3:15). Only a few passages bear directly on a "call to pastoral ministry," and these do not lay out an exact framework for recognizing such a call. Yet when we take them together, they do give us reason to expect that anyone who enters the pastoral ministry should do so only by means of a divine call.

We might begin our investigation by considering Hebrews 5. After the writer explains that "every high priest is selected from among men and is appointed to represent them in matters related to God," he insists that "no one takes this honor upon himself; he must be called by God" (5:1, 4). Note that although these priests were "selected from among men" and "appointed" to represent others before God, they had to be "called by God." Can we really imagine that God would do less for his new covenant people than he did for the old?

We don't have to imagine such an unsettling scenario, for we see the Lord doing in the New Testament exactly what he did in the Old. In Acts 13:2, Luke records that while the church at Antioch was "worshiping the Lord and fasting, the Holy Spirit said, 'Set apart for me Barnabas and Saul for the work to which I have called them.'" Paul accepted these heavenly marching orders and identified himself later as one who was "called to be an apostle" (Romans 1:1; 1 Corinthians 1:1; see also Galatians 1:15).

However, this old missionary never imagined that God's call would stop with him. That is why he told the Ephesian elders in Acts 20:28 that it was the Holy Spirit who had made them overseers, and that is also why he warned his protégé Timothy not to "be hasty in the laying on of hands" to set others apart for service (1 Timothy 5:22). It is as though Paul were telling the young pastor, "Make sure you know that a man is called into God's service before you endorse his ministry by publicly laying your hands on him. Be careful before you take such an important step!"

So, then, we can rightly ask, If God in the past specifically set apart men and women to serve his church, would he not do so in the present? I like what Charles Wagner has to say about this:

> It is incongruous to think that an ambassador would go to a country as a representative of his homeland without being sent. This is even more true in the ministry. One of the most vital areas of pastoral theology is that of the call to the ministry; the awareness of such a call is imperative. To go, without being sent, is to walk in failure.[4]

I believe that every one of us in the pastorate should be able to say, as did the apostle Paul, that our ministry is not from men nor by man, but by the will of God (see Galatians 1:1).

THE ROLE OF GIFTING

It is one thing to believe that God still calls specific believers into specific ministerial roles; it is quite another to recognize such a calling when it comes. If God does not call us with an audible voice, how are we to know for sure that we are called?

A big piece of the answer—but not all of it!—may be found in our personal gifting. That is, we must ask ourselves, "Am I gifted for the role of pastor? Has God equipped me to shepherd his flock? Do I fit the qualifications the Bible lists for anyone who wants to serve God in this way?" Regarding this element of recognizing God's call, Joe Stowell reminds us:

> In Ephesians 4, Paul declares that each one in the body of Christ has been given grace, i.e., a special enablement, "according to the measure of Christ's gift" (Ephesians 4:7). Paul follows this with an interesting statement regarding the ascension of Christ. He says that when Christ left this planet to function as our Advocate and High Priest in heaven, He "gave gifts to men." The [implication] is that when He gave us the task of carrying out the work of His church, He also graciously supplied

supernatural enablement for us to carry out the assign-
ment. In the midst of our insecurities, we must remember
that He empowers us with enabling gifts of ministry.

The gift of pastor/teacher combines two key elements
of local church leadership: the ministry of caring and concern combined with the indispensable ingredient of
instructing the flock in the truth of God and its ramifica-
tions for their lives. Those with the gift of pastor/teacher
are individuals who are particularly inclined toward the
needs of people and are committed to meeting those
needs not just through the ministries of personal resourc-
ing, but public proclamation.[5]

Jay Adams makes the same point:

> The important list of church office bearers in
> Ephesians 4:11 describes the Christian minister as that of
> a "pastor and teacher" (or perhaps, to convey the Greek
> text most clearly, a "pastor-teacher"). In this verse the
> minister's *teaching* is viewed as distinct (but not separate)
> from his *pastoral* duties. That is to say, the two works are
> distinguished by the use of two terms but not in such a
> way that two offices composed of different personnel are
> in view. Rather they are viewed as two distinct but insep-
> arable functions of one man who occupies one office.[6]

God does not call anyone into a service for which he or
she is unsuited. Yet we must be careful here! Would *we*
regard the oft-jailed, sharp-tongued, whirling dervish we
know as the apostle Paul as "suitable" for church ministry?
How about the apostle Peter? Tax-collecting Matthew? Yet
all these men really were gifted by God for the tasks and
roles to which he called them. As they were, so must we be.

A PASSION FOR MINISTRY

A second key component identifying God's call on our
lives to pastoral service is an unmistakable passion for
church ministry. It is not enough to possess the gifts that

would enable pastoral service. There must also be an unquenchable desire burning in the human heart to serve God in this way.

In his excellent book, *The Call*, Os Guinness explains, "Calling is the truth that God calls us to himself so decisively that everything we are, everything we do, and everything we have is invested with a special devotion and dynamism lived out as a response to his summons and service."[7] Note several words Guinness so carefully chooses: "decisively," "special devotion," "dynamism." Those called into pastoral ministry know they could never choose to do something else (not that they would want to). They know they are made for the pastorate like a fish is made for the sea, like a bird is made for the air.

If, for whatever reason, they try to do something else, they begin to sound a lot like the prophet Jeremiah when he tried to resign his commission to look for another calling:

> But if I say, "I will not mention him
>   or speak any more in his name,"
> his word is in my heart like a fire,
>   a fire shut up in my bones.
> I am weary of holding it in;
>   indeed, I cannot. (Jeremiah 20:9)

Although the prophet's ministry brought him nothing but ridicule and mocking, insults and reproach from those to whom he ministered, he found himself compelled to fulfill God's specific calling on his life. He could do no other.

The apostle Paul knew something of Jeremiah's intense ministerial imperative. His attitude is well expressed in 1 Corinthians 9:16, where he confessed, "I am compelled to preach. Woe to me if I do not preach the gospel!"

Pastors serving in the later centuries of the Christian era have made similar comments. The great Charles H. Spurgeon once told his ministerial students, "If any student in this room could be content to be a newspaper editor, or a grocer, or a farmer, or a doctor, or a lawyer, or a senator, or a king, in the name of heaven and earth let him go his way; he is not the man in whom dwells the Spirit of God in its fullness, for a man so filled with God would utterly weary of any pursuit but that for which his inmost soul pants."[8]

Several years ago a friend of mine, a seminary graduate who had not pursued full-time ministry, was asked to consider a pastoral position with a growing church. This man has strong teaching and leadership gifts, and he has used them extensively over the years in the several churches where he has been a member. He was at a point in his professional career at which he had begun to wonder if he ought to use those gifts in full-time church ministry. After several weeks of prayer, pondering, and earnest discussions with others, my friend decided against even interviewing for the position. Do you know why?

When he carefully examined the key biblical texts regarding church ministry, he began to notice one consistent element, an element largely lacking in his outlook. Read the texts for yourself and see if you can spot this make-or-break factor:

- "Here is a trustworthy saying: If anyone sets his heart on being an overseer, he desires a noble task" (1 Timothy 3:1).
- "Obey your leaders and submit to their authority. They keep watch over you as men who must give an account. Obey them so that their work will be a joy, not a burden, for that would be of no advantage to you" (Hebrews 13:17).
- "Be shepherds of God's flock that is under your care, serving as overseers—not because you must, but because you are willing, as God wants you to be; not greedy for money, but eager to serve" (1 Peter 5:2).

Did you see it? All three of these passages resound with the trumpet blast of passion for pastoral ministry. They express that passion in different ways, but the same intense desire for ministry surges through all three. As soon as my friend saw that, he knew that pastoral ministry wasn't for him. No great passion for the ministry rumbled in his heart. No intense desire. No overflowing joy at the thought of serving as a shepherd. My friend believed he possessed the gifts to do a good job in a pastoral role, but these lively words from the first century shocked him into realizing that God wanted passionate shepherds, not merely dutiful ones.

Consider the key words of these passages. Paul talks about someone who "sets his heart on" ministry, about someone who "desires" it. The first phrase translates the Greek term *orego*, which literally means "to stretch oneself, to reach out one's hand" and which came to mean "to aspire to, to strive for, to desire."[9] The second word, *epithymeo*, means "to desire, to long for."[10] Through the use of these words, the apostle paints a picture of someone who yearns for pastoral ministry as a deer pants for cool water.

The writer of Hebrews changes the vocabulary but not the sense. He contrasts the "joy" (*chara*) that pastors should experience (like that of the disciples when their risen Lord appeared to them; see Luke 24:41) with the "burden" (*stenazo*, to "*sigh, groan* because of an undesirable circumstance"[11]) they would be forced to bear if their sheep acted in stubborn and contrary ways. This is not the language of bare duty but of a full and overflowing heart!

Peter picks right up where the writer of Hebrews leaves off. He tells his readers that no one should pastor out of sheer duty ("because you must"). On the contrary, they are to shepherd God's flock because they are "willing" or even "eager" (*prothymos*, meaning "*willingly, eagerly, freely*"[12]) to serve. In other words, God requires passion of those who serve his flock as undershepherds. There must be no half-hearted, lukewarm, tepid forays into the pastoral ministry to try it on for size to see if it might fit. None of that for Paul! None of that for the writer of Hebrews! None of that for Peter! They all demand overseers with passion for the task, and no one else.

This is where that Funny Interior Feeling comes in. Because I have been long infected with the FIF disease, I can't see myself doing anything other than pastoring. It's not that I *can't* do anything else. At one time I did work as a mechanic, but I am not a mechanic. I have also done carpentry, but I am not a carpenter. I am a pastor—that is my identity.

Someone on my staff once asked me, "How do you know you're called?"

"Because," I replied, "you can't see yourself doing anything else."

"Well, I can't *do* anything else," he admitted. "I took time out of my life to go to Bible college and seminary, so there is nothing else I can do."

"But that's not the issue," I insisted. "Can you *see* yourself doing anything else? That's the defining mark. You can't allow your decision to be dictated by the thought that you can't earn a living unless you do this." That man eventually left the ministry. The truth was, he could see himself doing just about *anything* else.

Erwin Lutzer once wrote, "I'm disturbed by those who preach and teach without a sense of calling. Those who consider the ministry to be one choice among many tend to have horizontal vision. They lack the urgency of Paul, who said, 'Necessity is laid upon me.'"[13]

I too am disturbed by those who try to pastor without ever having received God's call to do so. Such attempts cheapen the God-ordained nature of pastoral work. I agree with John Henry Jowett, who warned, "If we lose the sense of wonder of our commission, we shall become like common traders in a common market, babbling about common wares."[14]

As a general rule, we feel most fulfilled when we minister in the area of our gifting, passion, and calling. When we leave that area, we often grow frustrated. No wonder the pastoral dropout rate is so high! Charles Bridges was right when he wrote:

> We may sometimes trace ministerial failure to the very threshold of the entrance into the work. Was the call to the sacred office clear in the order of the church, and according to the will of God? . . . Where the call is manifest, the promise is assured. But if we run unsent, our labours must prove unblest. Many, we fear, have never exercised their minds upon this inquiry.[15]

Amen. A little exercise never hurt anyone—and it has saved a number of people from serious injury down the line.

THE PERSONAL AND CORPORATE DIMENSIONS OF GOD'S CALL

Let's say that you believe you are gifted for the pastoral ministry. You also feel a passion for the work; you can see yourself doing nothing else. Does that mean God is calling you to the ministry?

Maybe, and maybe not.

When God calls someone to be a shepherd of his flock, he generally doesn't do it in isolation. Personal conviction is an absolute requirement, but the church's voice needs to be heard as well. Erwin Lutzer rightly says, "God's call is an inner conviction given by the Holy Spirit and confirmed by the Word of God and the Body of Christ."[16]

God's call involves both inward conviction and external confirmation by the church. When we study God's call of Paul, we notice immediately the deep involvement of the body of Christ. Paul didn't bust down the church doors at Antioch and proclaim himself a missionary. It is significant that he and Barnabas received their call during a church service, when the congregation was "worshiping the Lord and fasting" (Acts 13:2). Notice also to whom Paul's call was announced: "Set apart for me Barnabas and Saul for the work to which I have called them." The Holy Spirit said those words to the congregation, not merely to a solitary Paul or Barnabas. It was as if the Holy Spirit said, "Listen to me, my flock. I am calling two men among you to serve me in a special way. Set Barnabas and Saul apart for this work." This way Saul knew about his call, Barnabas knew about his call—and the entire church knew about both. That's why they confirmed the call by placing their hands on the pair and sending them off.

It would be scary if we had to depend solely on a person's inner conviction to know whether God had called that one to shepherd his sheep. For example, my fifteen-year-old son came home from camp last summer and announced, "I think God might be calling me to ministry, but I don't want to be a pastor." We talked about sports ministry and I introduced him to some representatives of Athletes in Action and a few other alternatives. Then I said, "If God doesn't give you a conviction to be a pastor, whether it be a youth pastor or whatever, then don't pursue it. But if God is showing you he wants to give you a life in ministry in some other area, then let's confirm that and take some steps to further your movement in that direction."

My son had heard a great motivational speaker at that camp, so his conviction may come or go. Who knows? But we don't have to depend merely on a fifteen-year-old's "gut feeling" to recognize God's call. I know if God is truly calling my son into ministry, the church will eventually confirm it. That's how God does things.

In a celebrated Lyman Beecher lecture, professor John Henry Jowett once declared:

> I hold with profound conviction that before a man selects the Christian ministry as his vocation he must have the

assurance that the selection has been imperatively constrained by the eternal God. The call of the Eternal must ring through the rooms of his soul as clearly as the sound of the morning bell rings through the valleys of Switzerland, calling the peasants to early prayer and praise.[17]

Such "assurance," however, comes only when a person's passion for ministry is enthusiastically confirmed by a body of believers. God uses the confirmation of his body to transform a personal call into the compelling force in a pastor's life.

A SCRATCH-N-SNIFF VOCATION

If I didn't know that God has called me to be a pastor, I wouldn't even get up some mornings. His call is what drives me. Being a shepherd is tough, unglamorous work. No one who understands the reality of pastoring would ever choose it apart from God's call. People might daydream about becoming a great leader, but few ever fantasize about doing a shepherd's messy work.

That is not to say that it can't be done, of course. I suspect that a lot of people enter the ministry because they don't understand who a shepherd is and what a shepherd does. They think it would be such a neat thing to take up a staff. By gazing at beautiful paintings of barnyard scenes that look so quaint, so peaceful, they nurture a romantic view of the pastorate. Yet one thing is true of every barnyard. Barnyards stink. These pictures might come closer to reality if they came in scratch-n-sniff versions.

It's too bad we can't come up with a scratch-n-sniff picture of the pastoral ministry. If we could, a person might think twice before entering it. It's a difficult life. It's blessed, to be sure, but it can be very hard—and unless God has called you to it, you should never pursue it. As Erwin Lutzer notes, "I don't see how anyone could survive in the ministry if he felt it was just his own choice. Some ministers scarcely have two good days back to back. They are sustained by the knowledge that God has placed them where they are."[18]

MY PERSONAL CALL

I received my call to the pastorate at age sixteen in a strange way. I was working at a Christian youth camp but was not following the Lord. In fact, I had no desire to follow him. But I taught horseback riding and thought it was a great way to spend the summer.

Then one night I heard a great speaker. I don't remember who he was, but I instantly knew I was to be a pastor. My parents were ecstatic when I wrote to tell them the news, but by the time I got home, I said, "I don't know what I was thinking. There ain't no way."

You see, I had never known a pastor whom I respected. Most of them seemed like the "geeks" of the kingdom. They were good, faithful men, but I didn't know one pastor who was athletically inclined. They all tended toward the uncoordinated, chubby set. So I ran as hard as I could away from that call . . . and from God.

When I returned to the Lord at age twenty, I knew immediately what I was supposed to do. No doubt about it. People would tell me, "You should be a youth pastor first," but I always replied, "Nope. God called me to be a pastor. I don't want a stepping-stone. He has called me to be a pastor."

When Susan and I began dating, my call is one of the first things we discussed. We were traveling together with a Christian music group, but God had not called me to be a full-time musician. He had called me to be a pastor, and she needed to understand that. Could she be willing to be a pastor's wife? Glory to God, she was.

Once we were married, we asked God to allow us to pastor with Village Missions, a group that targets small towns and opens up closed churches. We had prayed and talked about what it would be like to pour our lives into a small community of people. It's the only specific vision of ministry I ever had.

We were supposed to open a church in upstate New York, but before we arrived my home church asked me to be its full-time, interim pastor. The church had shrunk from an attendance of 250 to about 75, and the deacons wanted me to help get it on an even keel so they could call someone else. We stayed three years, then thought, *Maybe this is the time.* We called Village Missions and said, "Can we reactivate? The church here has grown and is stable." But nothing came of it.

That's when we received a call from a church in New Jersey with some problems of its own. This church of 150 to 200 in a middle- to lower-middle-class town of 6,000 had built a 500-seat auditorium—by amassing a debt of $600,000. Would I come to be their pastor?

"We really want to go with Village Missions," I said. We even called another agency, but the timing didn't seem right. So Susan and I said, "Well, God must be making it clear that we're supposed to go to New Jersey." So off we went to serve a hundred-year-old church with a new building and a massive debt.

A group of church consultants once created a chart of the character qualities necessary for a "turnaround pastor." I possess only about half of them. You're supposed to have a strong stomach for confrontation; it makes me sick to my stomach. I could have asked, "Lord, why in the world would you have me do this?" I still don't fully know the answer to that question, although Susan says I get bored when everything runs smoothly. She knows I like the challenge of bringing hope to people in pain. I really hurt for sheep who have been beat up.

Through all this, God never let us fulfill our vision with Village Missions. While it was the only specific ministry vision I ever had, it never bore fruit. That has always intrigued me. The main thing is that God called me to pastor. That's the extent of my call, a call identified in the church that ordained me and which continues to be confirmed today.

I have been in ministry now for more than twenty years, and I can honestly say I have a growing delight and passion to live out my call as a pastor. I have no distractions and no competitors for my time, for my strengths, for my allegiance, for my gifts. I have one passion that I have acted on with abandon for more than twenty years, and that is to be a shepherd, under God, for his people.

I never doubted that God called me to be a pastor, even when I served with Promise Keepers. Everyone knew that I was a pastor and that I would not stay in a parachurch ministry for long. People even sent me notes reminding me that I was a pastor. It's my whole identity. I am a pastor, and I want to follow only those things that are consistent with my calling.

CALLED TO BE SO WE CAN DO

Has God called you? If so, to what did he call you? Until you can define that, you're not in a position to minister. In short, what has he called you to *be* so that you can *do*?

Some time ago I interviewed a man for a staff position, but our conversation that day didn't last long. I performed the basic assessments: describe your gifts, your calling, and so forth. But when someone starts off by asking me to describe the benefit package and the salary range, I don't talk to him or her again. Unless I hear from somebody, "What's my role with the sheep? What unique thing would I be called to do? How would I fit in?" I'm not interested.

Pastoral ministry is not just a job. I've heard applicants immediately ask, "Will I have a secretary? Do I have to share? Do I get voice mail? Do I get a pager or a cell phone? Can you show me where my office would be, so I can see if it's big enough?" These questions have nothing to do with pastoral ministry, which comes down to this: Is God calling you to this particular flock? Can you sense that God is calling you to minister to this specific congregation?

That is the heart of God. That is Jesus standing over Jerusalem, weeping because the people were like sheep without a shepherd. The question is, Are these sheep whom God is calling me to love? If so, I'll spend my life for them.

The pastorate is both a calling and a lifestyle. Doctors know something of what this is like because there is never a time when they are *not* a doctor. I talked to a friend the other day who complained, "You know, I wish that just once we could sit down in a restaurant and nobody would interrupt to say, 'Hey, Doctor!'"

It does get awkward at times, especially as your kids get older. They often view the pastoral identity as an intrusion. The truth is, I *am* a pastor, and there is no time when I am not a pastor. It's who I am. It's my identity. That is how I am defined. I am a pastor.

This explains why I don't like being called "Preacher" or "Dr. Wagner." Those titles don't do a thing for me. "Glenn" is cool, but it does something special for me whenever someone calls me "Pastor." A distinctiveness about that word reminds me of who I am. It's not what I do that defines me; it's who I am. That, I think, is the essence of God's call.

The old Puritan Richard Baxter was on to something when he wrote, "The ultimate purpose of our pastoral oversight must be linked with the ultimate purpose of our whole lives. This is to please and to glorify God. It is also to see the sanctification and holy obedience of the people under our charge."[19]

Pastor. I like it. I really do!

GOD DOESN'T DO THINGS OUR WAY

God doesn't do things the way we would. The Lord goes to some coward hiding in a winepress and says, "I'm going to make you a mighty man of valor."

If we had handed Gideon a modern gifts and talents inventory, would he have ended up where he did?

God goes to some little shepherd boy and says to him, "I'm going to take you out of the sheep pens and make you the shepherd of my people Israel."

If we had been looking for a king, would we have searched in the pastures?

God goes to a murderer named Saul and says, "I'm going to make you an apostle to the Gentiles."

If we had wanted to commission a wildly successful missionary, would Paul have ever passed our screening criteria?

God goes to a big oaf named Peter, a fisherman with foot-in-mouth disease, and says, "I'm going to make you one of my apostles. In fact, you'll be the leader."

If we had been asked to disqualify one of the apostles, would we have picked Cephas or Judas?

No, God does not do things as we would. He even tells us, "my thoughts are not your thoughts, neither are your ways my ways. . . . As the heavens are higher than the earth, so are my ways higher than your ways and my thoughts than your thoughts" (Isaiah 55:8–9). Jesus adds, "Enter through the narrow gate. For wide is the gate and broad is the road that leads to destruction, and many enter through it. But small is the gate and narrow the road that leads to life, and only a few find it" (Matthew 7:13).

We should not try to enter in—either to eternal life or to pastoral ministry—by some other way, only by *his* way. When we comply, when we do things his way, the picture envisioned by Henlee Barnette more than three decades ago just might begin to turn into reality for us:

> A recovery of the theological doctrine of calling in the contemporary churches would transform them into revolutionary forces in a revolutionary age. Society itself would feel the impact of a prophetic faith and be brought more into conformity with the Kingdom of God on earth.[20]

Let it be so, Lord. Let it be so.

Chapter 9

THE GLORY OF SHEPHERDS

As a boy I often heard people say, "There is no greater calling in all of life than to be a pastor." Back then, both people inside and outside the church thought of the pastorate as the highest and most noble vocation possible.

I miss those days. Nowadays it seems that even church leaders are snubbing genuine pastors. Remember me telling about the message I preached in February 1998 to more than four thousand pastors on God's call to be shepherds of the flock? A few days later I received a letter from one of the attendees. He had been fired from his church because, he was told, "You're not a leader. You're a great pastor and preacher, but you're not a leader and we need a leader." That church had no problems with his vision, his preaching, or his caring for people. To this day the man doesn't know what critical quality he's missing.

I also heard from another pastor who took a profiling test to identify his spiritual gifts and talents. When the test identified him as a pastor, he lost his job. "I don't want pastors on my team. I need leaders," the senior pastor explained.

Clearly (and sadly) the days when pastoral ministry was exalted and esteemed have long since passed. Noting this, Pastor Jack Hayford wrote:

> During the 40-year span of my ministry, a radically diminished view of the social significance of "the ministry" has evolved. I remember how in mid-twentieth century North America some books about pastoral work warned the reader against the temptation of entering the ministry for the sake of the social prestige the position could provide. Today, such a remark would be seen as a joke. Yet multitudes are not laughing. They are the shepherds into whom God, at some moment in the past, breathed the promise wrapped in a call—a call to serve Him in a role of spiritual leadership.[1]

Hayford traced some of this decline of respect to infamous events in America's recent past: "Today's church leader lives in America's so-called 'post-Christian' era, in the cynical post-fallen-TV-evangelist setting. This era has shrouded ministry with a cloud of public doubt that has brought the once-designated *highest* calling to often be regarded as less than the lowest."[2]

Consequently, I meet numerous pastors who are beaten up, discouraged, and ready to quit—and I want to sound a loud note that declares unequivocally, "Thank God he called you to be a shepherd of his flock! Praise God you're a pastor!"

To those who ask, "Is pastoral ministry noble? Is it right to pursue becoming a pastor instead of being a leader?" I want to shout, "Yes! Never be ashamed that God called you to be a pastor. Never feel embarrassed that you were created to be a shepherd of the flock of God. Glory in your high position! Pursue it with all your heart! Never stop thanking God that he put you into the ministry!"

True pastors hunger for this type of encouragement; it resonates with their beaten-up, discouraged souls. That's why I want to help free them, however I can, to be the pastors God called them to be. One way to do that is to remind us all of the glory of shepherds.

FIVE REASONS TO GLORY

"Count your blessings, name them one by one," the old hymn encourages, and pastors should heed its good advice. Pastors enjoy a number of unique blessings that ought to recharge their spiritual batteries and reinvigorate their souls. It really is a glorious thing to be called a pastor! Allow me to sketch out five of the biggest reasons to exult in our divine calling.

1. God Has Entrusted You with the Pastorate.

When God called you to shepherd his sheep, he entrusted you with some of his most precious treasures. God not only believes in you but wants to bless you beyond your wildest dreams. He had something wonderful and specific in mind when he called you to be a pastor. Recall just a few of the priceless possessions he has entrusted to you.

- *Pastors are entrusted with the glorious gospel of God.* As a minister of Christ, you can declare with Paul that "the glorious gospel of the blessed God" has been "entrusted" to you (1 Timothy 1:11). Like Paul, you can say, "we speak as men approved by God to be entrusted with the gospel" (1 Thessalonians 2:4).

Meditate on that fact for a moment. You have been approved by God to shepherd his flock, and the good news of the gospel of Christ—the message of reconciliation with God, of eternal life, of pleasures at God's right hand forevermore—has been entrusted to you. It still sends shivers down my spine!

- *Pastors have been entrusted with the secret things of God.* Paul writes, "Men ought to regard us as servants of Christ and as those entrusted with the secret things of God" (1 Corinthians 4:1). Of course, we are not apostles, but pastors. We preach from the canon, we don't add to it. But when Paul talks about "the secret things of God," I think he has more in mind than his role as an agent of revelation. Paul was astonished and humbled that he had been chosen by God to proclaim a message "hidden for long ages past" (Romans 16:25). He marveled that God had called him "to preach to the Gentiles the unsearchable riches of Christ, and to make plain to everyone the administration of this mystery, which for ages past was kept hidden in God" (Ephesians 3:8–9). He rejoiced that the Lord had commissioned him "to present ... the word of God in its fullness—the mystery that has been kept hidden for ages and generations, but is now disclosed to the saints" (Colossians 1:25–26).

Likewise, the apostle Peter never got over his amazement that God had entrusted to him the same message about which the revered prophets of Israel had tried to "find out the time and circumstances to which the Spirit of Christ in them was pointing when he predicted the sufferings of Christ and the glories that would follow," the very message that even "angels long to look into" (1 Peter 1:11–12). Marvel of marvels—*that* is the message God has entrusted to *us*!

- *Pastors have been entrusted with the preaching of God's Word.* In Titus 1:3 Paul tells us that God entrusted him with not only the gospel, but more specifically, with its proclamation. "At his appointed season he [God] brought his word to light through *the preaching entrusted to me* by the command of God our Savior," he declares (italics added). Later, when he charges Timothy to "preach the Word," it is clear that the young pastor has received the same appointment (2 Timothy 4:2).

It is a solemn and breathtaking privilege to preach the Word of God! To think that we pastors have been appointed to tell others what God thinks—this alone ought to drive us to our knees in thanksgiving. Yet there is more.

- *Pastors have been entrusted with God's work.* We read in Titus 1:7 that an overseer "is entrusted with God's work," and in other texts we further learn that God considers us his "fellow workers" (1 Corinthians 3:9; 2 Corinthians 6:1). We pastors do not merely preach, marry, bury, counsel, administrate, and perform a thousand other tasks. *We are coworkers with God in the work of God.* Is there more noble labor than the work of God? Is there a greater colleague than God our coworker? What marvels have been entrusted to us!

- *Pastors have been entrusted with God's people.* The apostle Peter exhorts us, "Be shepherds of God's flock that is under your care ... not lording it over *those entrusted to you*" (1 Peter 5:2–3, italics added). God has entrusted to us the men and women, boys and girls, for whom Christ died. Every person saved by grace is a child of God, a bearer of the divine image, a royal priest, a temple of the living God in whom the eternal Spirit dwells. When we look at some of them we may see squabbling sheep, determined to wander and even wound the shepherd—but they won't always be like that. God has entrusted to us their spiritual care and training, and he expects his shepherds to fulfill their tasks faithfully and humbly.

God says to you, "You are the shepherd. These sheep are mine, but I want you to tend them for me." God has entrusted his sheep only to those he has called as shepherds. That's a place of honor. Amazing!

Of course, God also speaks directly to his sheep for our sake, telling them to "obey your leaders and submit to their authority. They keep watch over you as men who must give an account. Obey them *so that their work will be a joy*, not a burden, for that would be of no advantage to you" (Hebrews 13:17, italics added). No one else has been entrusted with God's own family—just us pastors. And God intends for it to be a joy.

- *Pastors have been entrusted with too many things to name.*
  I love both the precision and the "imprecision" found
  in Scripture. I am glad that the same Bible that can
  quote a certain prophet by name can also say, "there is
  a place where someone has testified ..." (Hebrews 2:6).
  In the tradition of the latter example I call your attention to 1 Timothy 6:20, where the apostle Paul tells his
  protégé, "Timothy, guard what has been entrusted to
  your care."

Who can name all the things entrusted to the care of a
pastor? Who could catalog the tasks, the duties, the expectations, the missions? The apostle knew better than to try, so
he simply said to his young pastor friend, "Guard what has
been entrusted to your care."

To whom else but a pastor has God entrusted all these
things? If one's calling can be measured by the worth and
the value of that which is entrusted, then the pastorate truly
is the highest calling, the noblest vocation possible. So Jack
Hayford can rightly exclaim:

> It extends deeper, wider and higher than any other sense
> of vocation, however valid, transcending even the inner
> urges of people who have lofty goals—those of scientists,
> writers, athletes, explorers and teachers. For, as shepherds
> who have been "called of God," we have answered an
> inescapably insistent summons; we are committed to
> serve a cause that pursues values earth can't quantify, and
> offers hope unto an era when earth will have vaporized.[3]

2. You Have the High Privilege of Being Identified As an Undershepherd of the Chief Shepherd.

The observation that Jesus calls himself "the good shepherd" (John 10:11, 14), that Peter calls Christ "the Chief
Shepherd" (1 Peter 5:4), and that the writer of Hebrews calls
our Lord "that great Shepherd of the sheep" (Hebrews
13:20) implies that all other shepherds serve under his
authority and mandate.

It ought to fill us with wonder that our Lord, the creator of the universe, not only calls us to be shepherds but identifies himself as a shepherd along with us. Jesus is one of us, even in our calling. He does not identify himself as "the Chief Landlord of the Pastures" or as "that great Owner of the sheep," but as a shepherd—greater than us, certainly, but one of us nonetheless.

I don't think Peter ever quite got over this. I doubt that it's mere coincidence that the man who called Jesus "the Chief Shepherd" also had a postresurrection conversation in which the risen Son of God charged him: "Feed my lambs.... Take care of my sheep.... Feed my sheep" (John 21:15, 16, 17).

We serve as undershepherds to the Chief Shepherd! Although we may never fully understand what a phenomenal privilege that is, we should exult in our privileged calling nonetheless.

3. Sheep Respond to a Shepherd.

Sheep respond to shepherds in a way that they never respond to mere leaders, CEOs, managers, administrators, or ranchers. I saw this principle validated once again just in the past few days.

Before I came to Calvary Church, the congregation had been through some difficult times. An ambitious building program had saddled the church with a multimillion-dollar debt, and for the past several years attendance had declined. When I arrived, plans were already under way for what is commonly called a "capital campaign." Since a fund-raising firm already had been retained, I went through the manual to take out anything I thought might harm the sheep. I refused to raise money and risk "conquering or manipulating the sheep," so we built the entire effort—"Moving Mountains: Our Faith Journey"—around prayer and fasting. Instead of preaching on stewardship, I communicated the vision and direction for our church. We asked God to bring a spirit of oneness to us and to move in his own powerful way. We set no financial goals other than to state our desire to start a course to become (and stay) debt-free. "Whatever God does financially is up to him," we said. "What we will do is minister to the sheep."

Before the campaign began, I sat with some business-people to explain what we were about to do. "Nobody can be asked for money," I told them. "There will be no categories of giving, no levels of giving. We won't ask even one person to give $10,000 or $5,000 or any other figure. We will merely communicate the need and give people clear and accurate information so they can pray intelligently. We will build up these sheep, not shear them. Our goal is that God will build within us a sense of oneness and hope, then take us deeper spiritually into what he has for us as a congregation." They thought I was crazy.

Nevertheless, for forty days our congregation prayed and fasted. One member of the staff wrote a devotional booklet dealing with various areas of spiritual life and growth. We held a twenty-four-hour prayer vigil and several other prayer gatherings. People gathered in homes to receive accurate information, to encourage one another, and to pray.

Two weeks before the end of the campaign, the church's prayer team, meeting in the basement under the sanctuary, fell on their knees in prayer as they lifted up their hands to God. At that exact moment people in the sanctuary responded to the ministry of our quartet by standing to their feet, some shouting "Glory! Hallelujah!" Please understand, this is a conservative church, and such things don't happen here. But it was a moment of incredible release and freedom and power.

In the middle of another service, we felt an overwhelming sense that we were to stop and offer a time of prayer and ministry for anyone who wanted to come forward. Dozens streamed to the front: a woman dealing with a recent miscarriage; another with cancer; several who said, "We came hoping that someone would pray for us, but we didn't know anybody well enough to ask."

During these days of prayer and fasting we have seen phenomenal things happen in marriages, in friendships, in the church—as well as significant spiritual warfare. God is doing marvelous things. What has happened in our congregation and among the sheep is far greater than any financial benefit we reap from the campaign.

Last night I announced the final figures, but first I spent some time talking about the marvelous things that had taken place in the flock. Then I made the announcement: that morning, we had received the largest single offering in the history of the church, while the faith commitments over the next three years set another record—all this despite the fact that the congregation is smaller now than it was during prior fund-raising efforts.

But the money really is secondary. God moved among his sheep, bringing oneness and hope and anticipation in what is classically called a capital campaign. Why? For one thing, I'm a shepherd with sheep to care for, not a CEO with a budget to meet—and sheep respond to a shepherd.

4. You Are Privileged to Watch God's Sheep Be Born, Grow, and Mature.

There is nothing like running into someone fifteen or twenty years down the road and hearing him or her say, "Pastor, you made a big difference in my life. I know it didn't look like it at the time, but it's because of you that I am serving God today." Testimonies like these can be year-makers.

For example, years ago I led a fellow to Christ shortly after his wife had come to faith. I had the privilege of baptizing not only him but his entire family. About a week ago he called to say, "I just wanted to let you know that you're my dad. You're the one God used to change my whole family and my whole life, and I'll never forget it." His family has suffered some heartache in the intervening years, but as he said, "Without the Lord, we never would have made it."

Or I think of another man whom I ran into recently. He let me know that he's still off drugs after a dozen years. He and his wife were heroin addicts, but today his marriage is together and two of his kids attend a Christian college.

I also think of the young people I dedicated as infants who now are graduating from college. I remember praying that they would come to Christ at an early age and never turn from the Lord. I know that they avoided much of the heartache and pain that others have suffered. How precious to realize God honors prayer!

Or I think of the woman who asked me to return for her funeral because I was there when her husband died and she knows I'll say the right thing. Or the man whose cancer went into remission, much to the amazement of his doctor, after we prayed for him. The list goes on and on.

It is this kind of hands-on ministry that I missed most when I worked with Promise Keepers. I was speaking to thousands of men every year, but I ached and longed for the opportunity to watch individual sheep grow and mature. Granted, great things happen in conferences, and I enjoy preaching at them. It's great to have someone come up and say, "Last year when you preached I made a decision and I've stayed with it." But during my time with PK I missed looking out over a congregation and seeing lives being transformed. When you witness the birth of a lamb, you want to see it become a sheep and ultimately reproduce itself.

Is there pain in trying to minister to those who are struggling? Absolutely. But as a pastor, you are privileged to see many victories as God's powerful and effective Word is ministered. There's nothing like it.

5. You Experience Unspeakable Joy Unknown to Anyone Else.

At times you sit with fellow pastors and start talking about "real stuff." You're close enough to them that you're not talking about facts, figures, numbers, or attendance records, but about life-changing ministry.

Susan and I have some friends like that whom we met early in our ministry. Whenever our paths cross, it's as though we've never been apart. As soon as we start talking, we get into the real stuff of life and ministry. These gatherings pulse with life and passion, even though there may be tears over a couple whose marriage is falling apart in spite of our best efforts to get them on track. We share a profound joy and delight in that kind of deep interaction, a momentous kind of rejoicing that happens only when you know *this* is what God has called you to do.

Pastors are the only ones able to share such a remarkable experience. I don't mean that only pastors can enjoy this type of deep camaraderie or that only shepherds are capable of such intense and joyful times of fellowship. But who else but a pastor knows the joy of helping God's children grow up in the faith? Who else but a shepherd knows the deep satisfaction of successfully guiding God's flock through valleys and over mountains, from summer through a long winter and back again? Someone who is not a pastor simply cannot understand what you are so excited about. But you can, can't you?

A BIT EMBARRASSED?

In Luke 9:26 we are warned not to be ashamed of Christ. That makes sense, for what do members of a royal priesthood (1 Peter 2:9) have to be ashamed about? On the other hand, neither are we called to defend our pastoral dignity or to strut our shepherdly glory. Quite the opposite.

I have found that divine glory is often found in the oddest places. It is a glorious thing to be called a shepherd of God's flock, but part of that glory is the divine calling to bear society's scorn. I wonder if we haven't forgotten about this. Sometimes I fear we go too far to be considered bright and respectable, even sophisticated. We've forgotten that part of a pastor's glory is the willingness to suffer reproach—to be thought of as a fool—for the name of Christ.

Charles Spurgeon, the preeminent British pastor of the nineteenth century, wrote in his famous *Lectures to My Students*, "We must try whether we can endure browbeating, weariness, slander, jeering, and hardship; and whether we can be made the offscouring of all things, and be treated as nothing for Christ's sake."[4]

The gospel we preach will never sound respectable to the world ... unless we have corrupted it. Let us always remember that "the message of the cross is foolishness to those who are perishing.... We preach Christ crucified: a stumbling block to Jews and foolishness to Gentiles.... The man without the Spirit does not accept the things that come from the Spirit of God, for they are foolishness to him" (1 Corinthians 1:18, 23; 2:14).

So where does the "glory" come in? Let's ask that question of some godly believers from the past. To this day, Moses is revered as one of ancient Israel's greatest heroes. Yet "he regarded disgrace for the sake of Christ as of greater value than the treasures of Egypt" (Hebrews 11:26).

The apostles walked with Jesus, performed mighty wonders through the power of the Spirit, and led thousands to Christ as they directed the infant church. Yet they gloried in none of this. Rather, when they were flogged by the Jewish leaders for speaking publicly about the risen Christ and commanded not to speak any more about their Lord, they "left the Sanhedrin, rejoicing because they had been counted worthy of suffering disgrace for the Name" (Acts 5:41).

Even Jesus Christ himself found glory in humiliation borne for the sake of the gospel. As Hebrews 12:2 tells us, "Jesus, the author and perfecter of our faith ... for the joy set before him endured the cross, scorning its shame."

We must come to see that part of a pastor's glory is being willing to accept and even to embrace the foolishness, disgrace, and shame of the cross. Thus God encourages us to go to Jesus "outside the camp, bearing the disgrace he bore" (Hebrews 13:13). Moreover, we are to bear this disgrace in a particular way. Peter says, "If you suffer as a Christian, do not be ashamed, but praise God that you bear that name" (1 Peter 4:16).

Praise God for bearing disgrace? Yes—as long as it's "disgrace" for our connection to Christ and not for some foolishness of our own.

Perhaps Paul can offer us a model. It may well be that there has never been a man who better understood both his own personal lowliness and his glory as a servant of the living God. On the one hand, Paul could say:

> We are fools for Christ.... We are weak ... we are dishonored! ... Up to this moment we have become the scum of the earth, the refuse of the world. (1 Corinthians 4:10, 13)

> For I am the least of the apostles and do not even deserve to be called an apostle, because I persecuted the church of God. (1 Corinthians 15:9)

> I am less than the least of all God's people. (Ephesians 3:8)

On the other hand, the same apostle could also say positive things about himself when the occasion warranted it:

> By the grace God has given me, I laid a foundation as an expert builder. (1 Corinthians 3:10)

> I do not think I am in the least inferior to those "super-apostles." (2 Corinthians 11:5)

> I am not in the least inferior to the "super-apostles," even though I am nothing. (2 Corinthians 12:11)

Was Paul schizophrenic? Didn't he know who he was? Or was he a manic-depressive, oscillating between self-loathing and self-confidence? I think the apostle from Tarsus was one of the sanest men who ever lived. He understood that "nothing good lives in me, that is, in my sinful nature"

(Romans 7:18), but he also understood that in Christ he had been elevated to undreamed-of heights and that God, by his grace, had commissioned him as an ambassador of heaven. He also knew, as Peter wrote, that "God opposes the proud but gives grace to the humble" (1 Peter 5:5).

I believe God intends for us pastors to be just a little bit embarrassed. God tells us, "I want shepherds," not "I want leaders," because built right into the fabric of the shepherd model is the humility so necessary to being a servant.

I have a Ph.D., but I don't like to be called "Dr. Wagner" unless I'm in some academic setting. I don't really like being called "Preacher" either, because "preaching" is something that I do. But "Pastor" reminds me of who I am. I never quite get used to it. Whenever I hear someone refer to me as pastor, I am always humbled to remember who I am and what I'm here for.

Now, I'm not suggesting that we insist that people call us by certain titles. But if we want to be in a place where God can use us, we need to stay humble—and the very image of a pastor-shepherd can help keep us there.

JOY AND GLORY

To be a pastor—not merely a leader, not merely a manager, but a true shepherd of the Lord's sheep—is a glorious calling that can fill our hearts with joy. There is no higher or more noble vocation on the planet.

In Jeremiah 3:15, God promised his people, "I will give you shepherds after my own heart, who will lead you with knowledge and understanding." Are you one of those shepherds? Has God called you to pastor some of his sheep? If so, he says to you, "Be a shepherd over my flock."

This is what God wanted in the Old Testament, and he still wants it today. There is no greater human role than to be a shepherd of God's people. So glory in it!

Part 3

LIFE IN GREEN PASTURES

Chapter 10

CONNECTED, RELATIONAL MINISTRY

About four or five years ago, I began having some disturbing conversations with pastors, Christian psychologists and counselors, and lay leaders. All of them were frustrated and saying, "What are we doing? Why are we doing it? Why does it seem that the more energy and money we put into the church, the less impact and effectiveness we have? Our churches don't seem to have the strength and the passion that God speaks of in the Scriptures."

One theme in our discussions continually resurfaced: our failure to build the church around the relationally driven model prescribed in the Bible. Instead, we have opted for a corporate model driven by programs and tasks. It's no wonder that the church is having such a negligible influence on culture, because personal transformation takes place largely through relationships.

At Promise Keepers I taught what we called the 80–10–10 principle. Basically it says that out of every one hundred people, 10 percent will change if you give them sufficient information, another 10 percent won't change no matter what you do, and 80 percent will change only in the context of significant relationships.

For example, the Surgeon General states that smoking is hazardous to one's health. Ten percent of the smokers read a brochure explaining the dangers of smoking and say, "Hey, that's bad. I'm going to quit." Another 10 percent read the same warning but say, "It doesn't really matter. All my friends are dead anyway," and go on with life as usual. What about the remaining 80 percent? They change only when a child says, "Daddy, I don't want you to die"; or a spouse says, "I really want you to be around"; or they learn that secondhand smoke can kill their children and grandchildren. That 80 percent changes only when they realize that their behavior threatens those they love.

This principle explains why God created the church. He intended it to be the ultimate community for life-transformation. God designed the church to be the primary setting in which we can be equipped and challenged to encourage and help one another.

For some reason, however, we have gravitated toward building models based on tasks rather than on relationships. That's why many people today say that the church feels more like a corporation than a community. The tragedy is that men and women in need depend on various support groups outside the church because we haven't figured out what it means to be community.

Even when we do learn some principles about community, we try to "program" them. We say, "Join the Barnabas Ministry," or, "Take our twelve-week *One Another* course." We insist on trying to fix our problems with programs because we don't understand that true caring can't be programmed. We can help mobilize caring individuals, but running a program does not equal biblical ministry. Our fundamental problem is that we don't *think* relationally, so we don't *act* relationally.

A genuinely caring church develops only when people understand who they are and what they are called to be in Christ. Effective churches universally emphasize connected, relational ministry.

METAPHORS OF RELATIONSHIP

The New Testament is all about relationships—between God and us, between us and others, between people of one race and another. The shepherd model fits perfectly into this connected, relational ministry pattern, but the leader model does not. In fact, many leaders must try to force themselves to be relational because their mind-set and identity is so disconnected from vital relationships. There is no shepherding without caring, but you can lead without caring. One NFL coach said, "The secret to leadership is caring, and the sooner you learn how to fake that, the better off you'll be." Unfortunately, that seems to be the attitude of many leaders in today's church.

But true shepherds don't have to "fake" caring; it's part of their identity. A genuine shepherd doesn't have to search for ways to artificially add caring to his makeup because caring is built into his basic nature.

If we focused exclusively on the metaphor of sheep and shepherd as a picture of the church, it would be enough to demonstrate the priority of relationships. But, in fact, the New Testament is packed with relational metaphors that instruct the church on what it is to be and how it is to act.

Nearly all of the terms God uses in the Bible to talk about the church are relational. Certainly the church has tasks to complete, but they all flow out of the relational model. The fact is, the New Testament couches virtually all its instruction about spiritual growth and development in relational terms.

For example, you can't read far in the New Testament without encountering dozens of "one another" passages.[1] God's people are exhorted to "love one another," "encourage one another," "be devoted to one another," "accept one another," "instruct one another," "greet one another," "serve one another," "bear with one another," "forgive one another," "submit to one another," "teach and admonish one another," "spur one another on toward love and good deeds," and "agree with one another." All of these commands are intensely relational.

Or consider a few of the various terms employed to describe the church. All of them are relational, emphasizing one believer's connection with another:

- The body of Christ (Romans 12:5; 1 Corinthians 12:27; Ephesians 1:23)
- The bride of Christ (Revelation 19:7; 21:2, 9; 22:17)
- Branches of the one true vine (John 15:5)
- Fellow citizens with God's people (Ephesians 2:19)
- Members of God's household (Ephesians 2:19)
- A holy temple built together (Ephesians 2:21–22; 1 Peter 2:5)
- A chosen people, a royal priesthood, a holy nation, a people belonging to God (1 Peter 2:9)

Even the Greek word translated "church" (*ekklesia*, "called-out ones") describes a community function. One scholar explains:

> In early Greece, cities were often ruled by pure democracy in which every citizen in the town would gather together to act upon matters of mutual interest. As they would be called out from their ordinary occupations to an assembly where they could vote, the word came to mean the result of being called out, or those who were thus assembled.[2]

God calls us "children" in his family, as well as "disciples," "brothers," and "sisters." We are "born" into God's family, but he also "adopts" us so we become "joint heirs" with Christ. All these terms and metaphors come out of personal connectedness.

We were designed to find strength in relationships. People talk about it all the time. Have you ever spoken with someone who met fellow believers from another country? If so, you probably heard a comment such as, "We didn't speak their language, and they didn't speak English, but immediately we sensed a deep connection with them because they knew Christ. We had the most marvelous time; it was magnificent. You wouldn't believe what it was like. If only you could have been there! Boy, that is really how it ought to be."

Such men and women have experienced the exhilaration that comes from being part of something bigger than they are. Others see the afterglow and say, "That's what I want. That's what I'm looking for."

Of course, the Bible also uses terms connected to task. But because we have adopted the corporate model in the American church, we have tended to be driven by these task words rather than the relational words. Yet the biblical truth seems to be that task flows out of relationship. So if we are performing a task poorly, it's probably the relationship that is at fault.

For example, could it be that evangelism is weak in American churches because we are relationally weak and thus have no compelling factor to motivate us to share our faith? Or consider our usual worship, which tends to be glib, trivial, and faddish. Might this reflect a failure to appreciate who we are as the people of God?

God, the One who is ultimate community, calls us all to live in community with him. And why is God community? Few people have proposed a better explanation than that offered by Jonathan Edwards more than two centuries ago:

> The Godhead being thus begotten by God's loving idea of himself and shewing forth in a distinct subsistence or person in that idea, there proceeds a most pure act, and an infinitely holy and sacred energy arises between the Father and Son in mutually loving and delighting in each

other, for their love and joy is mutual.... This is the eternal and most perfect and essential act of the Divine nature, wherein the Godhead acts to an infinite degree and in the most perfect manner possible. The Deity becomes all act, the Divine essence flows out and is, as it were, breathed forth in love and joy. So that the Godhead therein stands forth in yet another manner of subsistence, and there proceeds the third person in the Trinity, the Holy Spirit, viz. the Deity in act, for there is no other act but the act of the will.[3]

And this I suppose to be the blessed Trinity that we read of in the Holy Scriptures. The Father is the Deity subsisting in the prime, unoriginated and most absolute manner, or the Deity in its direct existence. The Son is the Deity generated by God's understanding, or having an idea of Himself and subsisting in that idea. The Holy Ghost is the Deity subsisting in act, or the Divine essence flowing out and breathed forth in God's infinite love to and delight in Himself. And I believe the whole Divine essence does truly and distinctly subsist both in the Divine Idea and Divine Love, and that each of them are properly distinct persons.[4]

John Piper, pastor of Bethlehem Baptist Church in Minneapolis, Minnesota, has spent a lifetime trying to catch the sense and implications of Edwards' theology. As Piper meditated over Scripture and Edwards' work, he encouraged his own audience to see that God

has loved his Son, the image of his own glory, with infinite and perfect energy from all eternity. How glorious and happy have been the Father and the Son and the Spirit of love flowing between them from all eternity!

Let us then stand in awe of this great God! And let us turn from all the trivial resentments and fleeting pleasures and petty pursuits of materialism and merely human "spirituality." And let us be caught up in the gladness that God has in the glory of his Son, who is the radiance and image of his Father. There is coming a day when the very pleasure that the Father has in the Son will be in us and will be our own pleasure. May God's enjoyment of God—unbounded and everlasting—flow into us even now by the Holy Spirit! This is our glory and our joy.[5]

We were created in the image of God—Father, Son, and Holy Spirit—which means that we were created for relationship. We are meant to live out and embody community. When we do, when our community functions as it should, people's needs begin to be met. Somehow we need to draw our focus back to this most basic of truths. The alternative is not very appealing.

THE CORPORATE MIND-SET

We often say that we want to bring people into a relationship with God, but how can a nonrelational model effectively communicate what it means to be in a relationship? The corporate model currently favored in the American church opposes the very thing we say we want to create. Corporations were never designed to create community.

It starts at the very top. The person we put at the helm of this enterprise thinks like a CEO, so even though he wants to bring people into relationship, even though he wants to build community, the very structures of the organization and his executive identity won't allow him to do so.

Since we've moved pastor and church out of the shepherd model and into an executive one, we see people refusing to commit to the local church. Why? Because the "corporate church" is not a community; men and women don't find vital relationships there. If they were honest, many church members would say, "I'm here only for the benefits. As long as the church meets my needs, takes care of my kids, and entertains me, I'll stay—but if it stops, see ya." The problem is, our corporate mind-set promotes a programmatic and task-oriented approach to ministry rather than a relational one, and corporations do not foster loyalty. When will we learn that it does little good to talk about relationships when our very structures are built around programs and tasks?

A LITTLE FABLE

Once upon a time in the city of Aarggh there lived a large family named Body. Poppa Body, Momma Body, and all the assorted little Bodys dwelt in an impressive house built on a corner lot near the center of town. The Body family had lived in that grand house for generations and had established quite a reputation for itself as a haven for outsiders down on their luck. Townspeople had learned over the years that they could always depend on the Body family to help out whenever bad times hit.

The Bodys could claim with pride that they had won the Neighbor-of-the-Year award more times than any other family in town—which is exactly what troubled Poppa Body one cold and drizzly morning. You see, for ten years straight the current Body family had failed to win the competition. Worse than that, these Bodys hadn't even placed in the top twenty-five.

"I don't understand it," Poppa Body growled to his wife through the house intercom. "We're the same Bodys we've always been. Why, just last week, didn't I put up that big billboard that said, 'The Bodys: A Family You Should Get To Know'? Can't anyone read anymore?"

"Well, dear," suggested Momma Body meekly, "maybe billboards aren't what people are looking for. Perhaps—"

"Yes, yes of course!" shouted Poppa Body. "Gotta keep up with the times. People don't read billboards anymore. I know what we'll do! It's time we put together a website. That should do it! Send up child number 3!"

"You mean Bobby," Momma Body corrected.

"Yes, yes, whatever," growled Poppa Body as he gazed off into the distance.

Soon Bobby Body bounded up the stairs to his father's executive office, knocked on its massive mahogany door, quickly entered, and snapped off the required salute. "Child number 3, reporting as ordered, sir," Bobby said.

"At ease, son," Poppa Body replied, "you know we're family here. Now, I think that we're falling behind the times. Can't have that. You know about computers?"

"Yes, sir," Bobby declared.

"Fine, fine," Poppa Body said. "I need you to build us a first-rate website. First-rate! People need to know why our family deserves the Neighbor-of-the-Year award. Can do?"

"Can do, sir," Bobby replied, then paused.

"Yes?" Poppa Body asked.

"Well, sir, I like the idea of the website, but . . ." Bobby began.

"YES?" Poppa Body demanded.

"Uh, well, it's just that . . . maybe we should concentrate on some other things that might have a bigger effect," Bobby began. "You know, Mrs. Franson really didn't like it much when we put up the big satellite dish; it cut off her view of the mountain. And the Bledsoes down the street, they used to come over for lemonade when it got muggy and hot; now they need an appointment three weeks in advance. And Terry Fisher just told me . . ."

"Enough!" Poppa Body then commanded. "Those approaches were fine and good for a simpler time, but you have to remember that we're on the verge of a new millennium! Progress! Efficiency! That's why we installed the new 900 MHz intercom system—it improves communication. That's why we have the little ones take the 'Introduction to Body Life' seminar—it gets them plugged in. By the way, I haven't seen child number 15 the last few days. What's up?"

"Her beeper's down, sir," Bobby replied. "A five-year-old just can't remember it's not a Frisbee."

"Well, run her through the 'Communication in the Family' seminar again," growled Poppa Body. "If you do, there's a bonus in it for you. Honestly, what has gotten into this family lately? Here we have the best equipment, the best programs, the best training seminars, and yet I can't even talk to child number 15—"

"Clarice, sir," Bobby interjected.

"—when I need to. Something needs to be done. But I've tried everything. What's left? How can we win the Neighbor-of-the-Year award when I can't even get my own family's act together? WELL?"

Bobby didn't say a word, though he thought he might know the answer. He had been reading the family archives, and he discovered that, somewhere along the line, the Bodys had ceased to function as a family and had started to act like a corporation instead. Of course, Poppa Body would never admit it; he talked too much about it being a family to see otherwise. But Bobby knew the truth. He also knew that they wouldn't be winning the Neighbor-of-the-Year award this year, either.

ISN'T THERE SOMETHING MORE?

In the Sermon on the Mount, Jesus declared, "You have heard that it was said to the people long ago, 'Do not murder, and anyone who murders will be subject to judgment'" (Matthew 5:21). Now, it's true that programs—"doing church"—can help us to avoid murder. We can learn to live by the rules, to become nice Christian persons; but Jesus isn't content with that. He continues, "But I tell you that anyone who is angry with his brother will be subject to judgment" (5:22).

Now, wait a minute, God! It's one thing to require that we abide by the rules—but asking us never to get angry is an entirely different matter! How can we do it? Here's how:

The Master set up a *transformational* model completely foreign to how his countrymen had been living. He gave a *relational* model to guide how people think, feel, and act.

I see the same principle at work in the church today. Until we embrace the relational aspects of knowing God and his heart, until we learn both to challenge and to encourage one another to deeper levels of interaction, we will never get to the human heart. We will spend our lives merely living by the rules.

Jesus also said, "You have heard that it was said, 'Do not commit adultery.' But I tell you that anyone who looks at a woman lustfully has already committed adultery with her in his heart" (Matthew 5:27).

"Whoa, there, Lord! Do you mean it's not enough not to sleep with someone's wife?"

"Yes, I do. It's an issue of purity of heart."

"But ... but ... well, how do I get *there*?"

I think this is the crucial lesson men in the Promise Keepers gatherings were learning when they began to experience relationships in a way they never thought possible. Where healthy relationships are developed, barriers break down and the Word of God gains access into the human heart and mind. Anyone can memorize the book of Philippians, but does this mean that Philippians has captured one's heart and life? Not likely, if it's memorized in isolation, apart from relationships. Only in relationships does life bump up against life and the Word of God get worked out.

More than once someone at a Promise Keepers conference came up to me and, with tears flowing down his cheeks, said, "You know, I've known Jesus since I was five years old; I'm now seventy-five. But this is the first time I have ever seen anything like this. This is the first time I have ever really worshiped." It wasn't so much the style of worship as its reality. You could *feel* it in the prayer, the interaction.

One man admitted, "I turned to my son, who is in his forties, and told him things in my life that I've never been able to tell even his mother, let alone God. I never knew you could experience that type of relationship." I heard such comments over and over again in Promise Keepers gatherings. Men gained the hope that things could be different, that they could develop transformational relationships. That's one reason I'm convinced that the relationally driven church is the transformational church.

This is the kind of relational ministry Paul had in mind when he wrote, "Therefore, my dear friends ... continue to work out your salvation with fear and trembling, for it is God who works in you to will and to act according to his good purpose" (Philippians 2:12–13). Note that the apostle addresses this message to his "friends," plural. And how are the Philippians to work out that salvation? Paul goes on to tell them to do everything without "complaining," without "arguing," and to "rejoice" with him (2:14, 18). All of those things are done in relationship and nowhere else. You complain to someone else. You argue with someone else. You rejoice with someone else. Paul cannot conceive of Christians working out their salvation apart from vital relationships with one another.

People today are asking, "Isn't there something more than merely going to Sunday school? Isn't there something more than just feeding the hungry? Isn't there something more?"

Yes, there is. Unfortunately, we tend to get "locked in" to patterns of thinking and modes of operation that stunt our spiritual, emotional, and social growth.

LOCKING IN

One of the elders at Calvary recently brought an intriguing analysis of the church to my attention. He says that the American church tends to lock in at various places on the spectrum of systematic theology and that this radically affects how we function.

For example, some Christians lock in at the point of their own justification. So if you schedule a testimony night, they will undoubtedly stand and declare, "I thank God that he saved me twenty years ago." John Piper talks about this orientation in *Living by Faith in Future Grace*. He observes that people like this always think about "the debt I owe."[6] Everything is in the past. These people can be described as nice Christians. The essence of their life is the rules and ritual. Just abide by the rules and maintain the form. They're justified, they're saved, they go to church—that's it.

Another group who wants a little bit more out of life locks in at sanctification. People who focus on their sanctification can also be defined as nice Christians, but they fall into rigor rather than rules. These people also define everything by the "now." The hallmark of their Christian life is: "God, fix my marriage now." "Lord, take care of my child now." "Father, give me a job now." The present drives them rather than the past. These people are rigorous in attending all the seminars and reading all the books on marriage and family. Knowledge is everything and is focused on "today." At testimony times they say things like, "Jesus is doing a wonderful work in my life."

A third group locks in at glorification. They pay more attention to the "future grace" that Piper writes about. What drives them is relationship. They talk a great deal about the grace to be revealed. The operative term in their life is "passion." There is a vibrancy and a vitality in their Christian walk. I think this is what men at Promise Keepers conferences started to see and experience. This group of people focuses on the future. At testimony meetings they say, with Paul, "No eye has seen, no ear has heard, no mind has conceived what God has prepared for those who love him!" (1 Corinthians 2:9).

Our problem is, most of our churches are built around groups 1 and 2. So when you start painting a picture of group 3 and begin talking about spiritual passion and vibrancy, you get a lot of blank stares. Nevertheless, as Peter and John declared, "We cannot help speaking about what we have seen and heard" (Acts 4:20).[7] When Paul writes, "I want to know Christ" (Philippians 3:10), he is talking about intimacy, experience of knowledge, vibrancy of passion. That's what the Greek word translated "know" means. The apostle puts the essence of the Christian walk in terms of relationship.

Let's bring this down out of the clouds for a moment. There are at least two ways I can live with my wife. On one hand, we can live together by *rules* and *rigor*. I can stay with her for fifty years on that basis, because on June 5, 1975, I said, "I do." We have a covenant. We can work on our communication skills and go away for romantic weekends to talk about all our hurts and secrets and to listen to marriage experts. That's one way to do it. On the other hand, I can live with her in a *relationship* that is so alive, so vibrant, that before she ever says a word, I know what she's going to say. We can be driven by an intimacy and a "can't help it" passion so that I simply can't keep her out of my thoughts, I can't stay away from her for long. There *is* something more than merely having a good marriage!

I believe this is what people in churches are looking for—relationships that make life worth living. A corporation can't give them what they want or need. A corporation can provide for groups 1 and 2, but not group 3. In our seminaries and teaching centers, we have locked into systems of theology that focus our attention on groups 1 and 2, but I think a new breed is starting to focus on group 3.

Still, there is a problem. How do we help people to shift to group 3 when everything we do in church locks in at groups 1 and 2? American Christians are willing to hear about relationship for their own personal benefit, but when we start talking about relationships for the benefit of others and for the glory of God, it gets quiet pretty quickly. Our world revolves around us, not others or God.

A while back I met with a group of pastors and Christian counselors about an idea for a seminar we wanted to pilot in Charlotte, North Carolina. The purpose of this seminar, which we tentatively called "Dare to Care," was to help our churches create community. The idea came out of some of these discussions, so I was hopeful that it would succeed.

It bombed.

Everyone liked the concept, but they were afraid of it. Pastors said, "If we do this, we'll have to undo everything we've been doing." Christian counselors said, "If you do this, you'll drive people into greater dysfunctionality. Besides, we'll go out of business if the church really functions as a community." Christian education directors asked, "What curriculum do I buy? What's the program? Is there computer software that helps me track this?"

Our idea was to give the church some tools to help its members think and live relationally. I think a total of three people registered, so we had to cancel.

NO COOKIE-CUTTER CHURCHES

If you are a pastor, you shouldn't be afraid of creating real community in your church. True, things will change, but isn't that what we want? Isn't that what we need? Survey after survey shows that people in every demographic group—whether Busters, Boomers, Builders, or whatever—are all looking for relationship. They define it in different ways, but they are all looking for a sense of community, a sense of belonging.

Nor do you have to be afraid that the principles that promote authentic community won't "fit" your church. The principles work regardless of a particular church's style or size. When I was teaching seminars for Promise Keepers, I said, "These principles hold true whether you have a church of fifteen, five hundred, or five thousand. Why? Because they are basic, fundamental principles designed to bring any people to maturity in Christ. You can lay these principles over any curriculum from any publisher, just so long as this philosophy of ministry stays in place. You can be urban, suburban, rural—none of this makes a difference because they are basic, biblical principles."

The idea is not for your church to become like my church. Rather, the Bible offers us some core principles that will revolutionize our churches if we allow them to do so. The principles will work themselves out differently depending upon our context, distinctives, and the like. The one thing that is nonnegotiable is the focus on relationships.

Churches who equip themselves to foster deep relationships may look quite different from one another because of the various regions, giftings, ages, and socioeconomic ranges they reflect. But they will look even more different from what they would have been had they continued to follow the corporate model!

BE, THEN DO

The first three chapters of Ephesians offer a solid, shining ecclesiology of the people of God. We were chosen in Christ before the creation of the world, Paul tells us. We were also adopted as God's children. We have been redeemed, forgiven, and granted an eternal inheritance in heaven. We enjoy free and unhindered access to the Father through Christ, in whom we are being built into a holy temple. We are all members of one body, having been connected to a power that can do immeasurably more than all we ask or imagine.

After this ecclesiastical tour de force, Paul exhorts us "to live a life worthy of the calling you have received" (Ephesians 4:1). So what calling does Paul have in mind? Is it self-actualization? Is it a technique to help us feel better about ourselves? No. It is a full-blooded understanding of who we are as the people of God.

I remember discussing with other leaders at Promise Keepers the best way to address the sin of racism in the church. One group wanted to stress the *imago dei*, the idea that all people are created in God's image. That's a social concern, the issue of the dignity of human life, and even non-Christians can understand and recognize its importance.

But I thought an even more effective challenge to our constituency would come from our ecclesiology. A greater motivation for the Christian is the truth of who we are in Christ. Paul teaches, "There is neither Jew nor Greek, slave nor free, male nor female, for you are all one in Christ Jesus" (Galatians 3:28). Later he reiterates, "Here there is no Greek or Jew, circumcised or uncircumcised, barbarian, Scythian, slave or free, but Christ is all, and is in all" (Colossians 3:11). Our common identity in Christ is the great leveler, the one thing that can eradicate racism from our churches!

Being must precede doing. Activity flows out of relationships. While the corporate model says, "If we do right, eventually we will be right," the biblical model insists, "Be right, and you will do right."

REPENT AND TURN

We pastors and lay leaders need to repent for institutionalizing and programmatizing the church. We have removed or hindered its key relational aspects, while the model of the church that God endorsed and designed—the flock of God, the family of God—centers on relationships.

We must first admit that we will never have a relational model of ministry (transformational in its very nature), unless we bring the church's structures into line. Then we must come to grips with the reality that, apart from a vital relational dynamic, we will continue to stunt our spiritual growth. Spiritual giants do not grow out of stunted relationships.

It comes down to this: A leader model cannot take us where we want and need to go, but a shepherd model can and will. It always has.

I tell you the truth, the man who does not enter the sheep pen by the gate, but climbs in by some other way, is a thief and a robber. The man who enters by the gate is the shepherd of his sheep. The watchman opens the gate for him, and the sheep listen to his voice. He calls his own sheep by name and leads them out. When he has brought out all his own, he goes on ahead of them, and his sheep follow him because they know his voice. (John 10:1–4)

Chapter 11

BUT DOES IT WORK?

My unwavering conviction is that if the Bible gives us a pattern for doing something, that pattern will "work." Because of this, we need not give lip service to a concept solely because it is taught in Scripture, then look elsewhere for something that actually delivers the goods.

For this chapter I interviewed five current pastors and one former pastor who strive to "put legs to" the shepherding model outlined in this book.[1] Their churches vary widely in size, location, age, congregational makeup, and personality, but they all share one thing in common: They have opted for a shepherd orientation rather than a corporate one. Their experiences illustrate how the shepherding model "works" in various contexts to exert a powerful influence on the communities they serve.

Allow me to introduce you to these shepherds and their flocks.

Glenn Blossom is pastor of Chelten Baptist Church outside of Philadelphia. Chelten attracts about seven hundred worshipers each Sunday. The church began about a century ago in a working-class community of Philadelphia's Germantown area but moved in the early 1960s to what was then a more rural community; today it can be characterized as middle to upper-middle class. Glenn came to Chelten on the first Sunday of November, 1974.

Colonial Church of Edina was founded in a first-ring suburb of Minneapolis just after the Second World War. **David Fisher** is its third senior pastor, following men who served in that role for seventeen and thirty-two years, respectively. Think of Pilgrims, Puritans, and New England, and you will have a fair idea of the style found at Colonial. It grew to be a church of over one thousand by 1960, and today it has a membership of three thousand, though actual attendance varies widely, depending on the time and season of the year. Most of its members—who prefer to describe themselves by the term *renewed* rather than *evangelical*—come from mainline Protestant churches, especially Lutheran, with "a smattering of Catholics," according to David. In 1996 David published an insightful book titled *The 21st Century Pastor*.

Rick Kingham recently took the reins as senior pastor of Overlake Christian Church in Kirkland, Washington, a prosperous suburb northeast of Seattle. Overlake, which attracts about five thousand worshipers each Sunday morning, was listed by Tom Telford in his 1998 book *Missions in the 21st Century* as one of the top twenty-one missions-minded churches in the United States.

In 1980 **John Piper** left the world of academia to pastor Bethlehem Baptist Church, a flagship congregation of the Baptist General Conference. Bethlehem sits under the shadow of the Hubert H. Humphrey Metrodome in downtown Minneapolis and can be seen from I–35W, which connects the city's north and south suburbs. When John first came to the church, attendance hovered around three hundred and its membership was graying and dying. Sunday attendance now averages about fifteen hundred, and the church attracts a lot of younger people, many from local colleges and seminaries. Away from his church, John is probably best known as the author of several God-soaked books such as *Desiring God, Future Grace: The Purifying Power of*

Living by Faith, The Supremacy of God in Preaching, The Pleasures of God, and *A Godward Life.*

Russ Rosser is the longtime pastor of the First Baptist Church of Flushing, New York, a historic congregation dating back to 1857. The church was founded that February by an Episcopalian graduate of Harvard who came to Christ in August 1856. With a heart for immigrants and a special passion for the Irish who were pouring into New York City, he set a pattern for church outreach that continues to this day. For example, in the 1960s First Baptist opened its doors to the Chinese community, while in 1978 it became a multilingual congregation with a deep commitment to reaching the many ethnic peoples of Flushing. Within walking distance of First Baptist are 100,000 people who hail from 135 countries and who speak 108 different languages. The church reflects that diversity, with approximately sixty languages spoken by its members. First Baptist worships in Spanish, Mandarin, Cantonese, and English, and has outreaches to Indians who speak Telugu and Filipinos who speak Tagalog. Some of my fondest memories are of my visits to Russ's new members class, jammed into his office with all the others, while he sat on his desk, orchestrating the whole overwhelming scene.

Before **Joseph M. Stowell III** became president of Chicago's Moody Bible Institute in 1987, he pastored the Highland Park Baptist Church in Detroit, having served churches in Indiana and Ohio before that. Joe is a third-generation pastor, following in the footsteps of his father and grandfather, godly men who he says influenced him more than about anyone else. Although Joe no longer pastors a church, a shepherd's heart still beats in his chest, and he insists he'd much rather be addressed as "Pastor" than "Doctor."

Now that you've been introduced to these shepherds of the flock, listen to the answers they gave to several key questions that I asked.

Q: How would you describe what a pastor is and does?

Glenn Blossom: "A pastor is the shepherd of the sheep. Three words are used interchangeably: He is an elder, a bishop, and a pastor. As a shepherd of the sheep, he oversees and must give an account of the souls in his care. He is the person who sits at the gate. It is the call of the pastor to lay down his life for his sheep. That works its way out in every area of his ministry. He is obviously a leader, but he is also a feeder. He is a nurturer. He is a protector. He is a 'carer,' a 'discipler.'

"Paul in Colossians 1:28 writes as a goal 'that we may present everyone perfect in Christ.' So the shepherd knows the sheep by name. He gives personal care. That may be difficult in larger churches, but that doesn't mean he can't know a lot of those names. That doesn't mean the pastor can't press a lot of flesh. That doesn't mean he can't hold a lot of those sheep, that he can't be there at significant times. Nor does that mean he has to be there all of the time. But as a shepherd, he will know his sheep. He will know their hearts, where they've come from, where they're going, where they are—and then lead them along developmentally.

"If a person does not love people, then I find it hard to believe that that person has been called to pastoral ministry. The fulfillment of the law is loving God with all your heart, mind, soul, and strength and loving your neighbor as yourself. For some reason we have believed that pastors can be technicians, which is totally foreign to the models and the teaching of Scripture. I once knew a church staff person whose favorite phrase was, 'The ministry would be fine if it weren't for the people.' That was almost his mode of operation, to work with his computer . . . and I thought, *That's pastoral?*"

David Fisher: "I take the old, classical definition: A pastor is one who is in charge of the cure of souls, or the care of souls. God has placed a number of souls in my care, and at the end of time I'm going to give an account of that care. In the meantime I look for ways I can care for people's souls. I do that by teaching, by preaching, by relationships, by visiting people in crisis.

"My leadership of the church is understood as helping the church set direction and all that, but the substance of what we're about is being the *church*, not a *company*. It is my conviction that the mission statements of most churches talk far too much about what the church is going to *do* and not at all about what the church *is*. So our mission statement is really very simple: God calls us to be the church. We are a company of people who are called to be the church, which means that we are to live in the grace of Christ and to share that grace with each other, to care for each other's souls. We who are the clergy are the primary 'soul-carers.'

"My predecessor was a classic pastoral shepherd, who was also a first-rate visionary and a very strong leader. He was from New England and had graduated from Harvard and Union Seminary. So he had that old congregational, Puritan, high-up-in-the-pulpit view of leadership. He led the church in powerful ways, but he never stopped thinking of himself as a country pastor. Two days a week he did all the hospital visitation. He would visit anyone, not only members, but anyone who wanted a visit. It took him two entire days a week to do this. Eventually he hired an assistant, a woman who came to be known as the church mother. She is now seventy-two years old but is still on staff. She's our Director of Pastoral Care. She knows everyone's name. She loves everyone, and everyone loves her.

"If you ask people what this church is about, pastoral care always gets put way up top. They mean by that various things, but most of all it means, 'Somebody here loves me.' When I came here, the first sentence out of my mouth on Sunday morning was, 'I've come here to care for your souls.' You could have heard a pin drop, because that's what they had become accustomed to. In a big church that just gets people's attention. So that's what we go about doing.

"We don't have a lot of specialists. We have four generalists who are pastors to the whole congregation. A lot of pastoral work gets done; I do a lot of it. We have a woman who will die before this day is over; two of our pastors have been to see her today. Two weeks ago all four of us went and made all the hospital calls together because we had three people who were dying. Pastoral work is a priority of the congregation. I don't know of any other church of this size in which that's explicitly the case. So this is a great place to work, to be a shepherd. I am expected to lead, and I do, but it is a by-product of being a shepherd."

John Piper: "What the pastor does is going to vary tremendously depending on his situation. There are about as many patterns of daily engagement with people and world and culture and unbelievers and missions as there are pastors.

"Still, I would say that the *poimen*, the shepherd, is one who feeds God's sheep. 'Do you love me, Peter? Feed my sheep.' The food is the Word. 'Man shall not live by bread alone but by every word that comes out of God's mouth.' So I think that a pastor is first and foremost a 'truth broker,' to use David Wells's phrase. But to keep our metaphors consistent, let's just say that the pastor is the one who feeds his sheep daily and weekly with biblical truth.

"But that has to be done out of a heart passionately in love with that truth and in love with that God, and out of a heart that models the transforming power of that truth. So what my people need most (as the Puritans said) is my personal holiness. Or as Spurgeon said, 'My people come to see me burn.' I also think of the call for Timothy to be an example to the flock of righteousness and faith and goodness. We are to stand before our people as those who not only point the way but who lead the way in the way we live, in the kind of risks we take with our lives—the kind of lifestyle we live, the way we give, the way we handle our money, the way we lead our families. That's why I think family issues and the biblical criteria for elders are important. They are all life issues that we must model for the people.

"I think elders are expected to govern well. Therefore, we must have some semblance of a gift for figuring out structures and ways that help our people love each other and the lost. I also think that we should have a prophetic dimension to us that trumpets the wider issues of making an impact on our culture and reaching the nations with the gospel.

"Maybe the last thing would be that a shepherd goes out and finds the lost and heals the legs and helps the sheep when they are down. He helps the weak and the broken and the dying. Last Sunday my wife woke me up thirty minutes into my afternoon nap. I was dog tired when she said, 'I wouldn't normally do this, but Marvell says Esther's asking for you, so I thought you'd want to talk to her.' So I talked to Marvell, the daughter, and then got in my car and went to help Esther die. I believe that's what a pastor should do. Those of us who have big churches don't do as much of it as maybe we once did, but we must do some of it. If every once in awhile we do that, if we sit at a bedside helping a family walk their wonderful mother through death, the news gets out. I was late for the service last night, and people knew why."

Russ Rosser: "A pastor in an urban, multiethnic, ever-changing community needs to be a shepherd, but also a leader in equipping and training new believers to prepare them to do the work of the ministry. Oftentimes as soon as you have them trained and equipped, they move to the suburbs or to a country of their origin or to some other part of the city. As a result, you are constantly not only shepherding people who are new believers but also providing administrative leadership in the congregation because of the quick-changing movement of people who come and go. It takes a great deal of administrative strength in the urban world because laypeople in their mature years are usually not available; they have already moved away."

Joe Stowell: "When I hear the word 'pastor,' I always think of a shepherd. I think of people-orientation, of one who gives himself to the needs of the sheep. I think of one who leads people to their growth and their gain as well as to God's glory in their lives. I think of sensitivity, of tolerance. I think of patience, of love. It's about relationships, not about power. It's about ministry, not about the platform on which I stand. It's about touching people's lives, not about having people touch me. It's about celebrating and encouraging other people, not seeking celebration and encouragement from others. The word 'pastor' drives me in the right direction. It drives me out of myself and to other people.

"I'm a third-generation pastor, or at least I was before I came to Moody. The people I admire most, like my father and grandfather, were pastors. Just the other day someone said to me, 'Pastor Stowell . . . oh, I'm sorry . . . *Dr.* Stowell.' I corrected him and said, '*Pastor* Stowell is the highest thing that you could call me.' 'Pastor' is a word of giving, of caring, of relationship, of ministry. I have always felt that 'pastor' is by far and away the most wonderful identity someone could have. If I had my druthers, I would be called 'Pastor' all the time."

Q: How do you let your people know that you care for them?

Glenn Blossom: "One of the ways I communicate my care for my sheep is by being accessible. People somehow have this view that I'm a very busy person. I believe anyone worth his or her salt is busy, but I don't want that communicated to my people. I want to be available to them.

"At the same time, they need to understand that I live with structure; everyone needs to live with structure. Still, although I have other appointments, meetings, study time, or whatever, I want them to know that I'm available. I find the best way to do that is to be with them as much as possible. For example, I try to go to all the Sunday school parties or church functions. We just had the senior adult meeting today, and even though I wasn't staying for lunch, I went around to every table and said 'hi' to everybody there. I talked to them for a couple of moments, looked them in the eyes, and hugged them. I believe in hugs. I'm a big hugger. I believe in touch; it's not only 'high tech,' but 'high touch.' All that is affirming what Jesus did. He touched people, prayed with them on the spot.

"I am also nearly the last person to leave on a Sunday morning. After I have stood at the door and people have left, I then turn around and go back into the auditorium and say 'hi' to as many people as I can.

"Finally, I try to be there, if I can, at the moment of crisis. That is very significant, and quite frankly, that's when people look for you. It makes a significant difference to them that you have been there when they needed you."

David Fisher: "I spend one afternoon a week in the hospitals. I don't visit everyone; I visit people who are in the constituency of the church. That doesn't work as well as it used to because people are in and out of the hospital faster these days. Several times a year I go with our Director of Pastoral Care and visit all our people who are in nursing homes (about fifty). I make it a point to go to a place where some twenty of our elderly live to hold Christmas Bible studies and Lent Bible studies. I'm only seeing one hundred people a year, tops.

"I'm careful about the language I use. You have to use appropriate language, gestures, symbols, and all. That lets people know what it means to be the church. I talk a lot about the soul and soul care. I never get through a sermon without somehow making it a church event. I'm careful about the illustrations I use. I'm never the hero of my stories, but I like to tell stories about soul care. I make it a point to tell stories that make me a real person. I let them know that I need care, too. In fact, one of my questions to the search committee before I came here was, 'Is it possible to be the pastor of a large church and have someone care for your soul?'"

Rick Kingham: "A lot of pastors use the pulpit primarily as the place for teaching the people, but I use the pulpit primarily for shepherding the people. If you shepherd the staff persons with whom you surround yourself, and you shepherd them in such a way that they can touch the people, then you are in fact touching everyone. That frees you to not feel so obligated to touch everyone individually, since you can touch them through communication. Here we do a lot of communicating, not just from the pulpit, but through letters, through newsletters, through videotapes and other things we use to help the body understand the vision and the heart of what we believe that God has called us to do as a church.

"I also make it a practice to see people who have huge decisions to make and those who are facing family crises. It's also important to celebrate significant events. So one of the priorities for my schedule is fiftieth wedding anniversaries, weddings, funerals. I place a high priority on helping families.

"Even though we have five thousand people on Sunday, my wife and I still stand at the door of the church and shake hands with as many individuals as we can. Before the service I go out and move through the auditorium to shake hands with people. I'm very visible—I don't do the 'come in when the service starts' and all of that. I take my place, but the people have seen me for a few minutes before that.

"On occasion I'll stand down front and often be the last person to leave the building. I learned that from Henry Blackaby, who said that he felt God told him that a man of

God will not leave until every person who wants to see him has had the opportunity to do so. Obviously you can't do that every time, nor should you try, but people know that there are occasions when I will be available to them."

John Piper: "A pastor's care for his people will surely come out most regularly in the way he talks to them on Sunday morning. Do they hear a shepherd? Do they see and feel someone who is saying what he is saying because he's broken over their sin? Because he's aching over their marriages that are breaking up? Because he looks out on wayward children who have thrown away their faith or are living with someone, and their parents can hardly stand it? That will come out. They'll hear that in his tone of voice. They'll hear in his illustrations that he knows the pain in the congregation. There's a difference between a pastor who gives broad, sweeping, culturally relevant, theologically correct statements and one who is in touch with the hurts and sins that are out there.

"Also, are there seasons within the life of the church where the pastor's hobnobbing and not running away to a meeting? I say, 'Look, I'm here after this service to pray with anyone as long as you want to pray.' I'm there regularly for an hour after the service, dog tired, standing at the front, praying one after the other with people who come up. While maybe only three, four, five, or eight people want to do that, everyone heard me *offer* to do that. Everyone sees me standing there. They see me with my arms around people. They hear me praying with people.

"A third thing helps the people know that I care: We elders go to pray with people and anoint them with oil when they call us. We do that quite a bit. We try to piggyback them, if possible, to another meeting, like in the prayer room downstairs before or after a service. I attend these special times as much as possible.

"Then there are opportunities to speak at marriage retreats. I've just been asked by our couples group to speak next March at our couples' weekend event on a Friday night. So I can be there and talk about my marriage and share my life with a group of seventy to eighty people. Then the youth asked me to speak at their love banquet in May. I've done that every year for five years. I often go to the parties that I'm asked to attend. I used to conduct tons of marriages and a funeral every three weeks when I first came here (our congregation was old and dying). I haven't done a funeral now for months. Over the years our congregation has gotten younger, and layers of management have distanced me from some of these things, but I'm still at a lot of events."

Russ Rosser: "I communicate my care by being available to my people. Pastoral care is usually not done in homes or apartments, because people in the urban environment do not necessarily invite a lot of people into their homes; they are too small. One family I'm presently caring for has nine people, three children and six adults, living in a two-bedroom apartment. To go to their home would be impossible. So I make myself available to them at seven in the morning before they hit the subway, or in the early evening for counseling and personal ministry as they're leaving the subway and going to their apartments or homes.

"Our people continue to be amazed at my availability, as well as that of the pastoral staff. A couple new to the church came to me the other day. The wife first went to the Chinese congregation but was having difficulty understanding Cantonese. She speaks fairly good English so she started coming to the English congregation but basically could come only at night because she works during the day. Her husband, a Canadian, was without work for a period of time. They went through a very difficult crisis just this week, and I've met with her twice now, along with him last evening. We have spent at least three occasions on the phone. Both of them said as they left our meeting, 'We cannot believe that you were available to us; you barely know us.' I think the availability blows them away. That's where you have to begin with people who are coming out of brokenness."

Joe Stowell: "I think you communicate it in your preaching with a compassionate, sensitive spirit. Your applications, your illustrations show sensitivity to their needs, and you can talk about your heart for someone in your congregation.

"A second way to show caring is the pastoral prayer. I remember my dad telling me about some great man who was most loved because of his pastoral prayers. The people said it was like he put his arms out, wrapped the whole congregation in his embrace, and took them to the throne as he prayed for them.

"More practically, I think it's how you walk through the halls, how you walk among your congregation. It's how you give eye contact, smile, try to remember names. Most congregations have a pictorial directory, and if a pastor would pray daily through that directory, suddenly names and faces would become more important. If a pastor walks down the hall and says to someone who is not the Chairman of the Board, 'Hi, Bob, how are you doing? Hey, I prayed for you this week. I just want you to know that, although I don't know everything that's going on in your life, I prayed for you'—that echoes for miles. People have written me notes saying, 'When you stopped and shook my hand and said "hi," that made my day.'

"Another thing that's important is, when they are talking to you, don't look past them at who's walking behind. Don't say, 'Oh, hi, Bob,' as somebody is pouring out his heart to you. It takes discipline to look a person right in the eye, refusing to be distracted even if someone else comes up and says, 'Hey, Pastor!' Just keep looking at this person so he or she feels cared for in that moment. And if someone says, 'Will you pray for my sister?' make sure that you do, then write a note on Tuesday saying, 'I want you to know I prayed for your sister. . . .'

"By the way, you don't have to do this for all four thousand people in the church. On Sunday mornings and Sunday evenings before our services, I would go about ten minutes early, walk up the aisle, stop and lean against the back of the pew, shake hands, and talk to somebody sitting there. You don't have to shake hands with everyone. The very fact that you went out there and shook hands with five people, looked them in the eyes, and asked, 'How are you doing?' and maybe slapped them on the back—it was like you did that to everyone. It's simple and it's huge."

Q: How do you try to create community in your church?

Glenn Blossom: "We want to keep community needs in front of our people in as many ways as possible. One way I do that on Sunday is by mentioning people and their particular needs by name. Every Sunday, people know the prayer requests."

Rick Kingham: "We constantly use one of the apostle Paul's favorite metaphors, 'the family of God,' the household, the *oikonome*, the economy of the family. Almost everything we say around Overlake is covered by those sorts of phrases. We talk about the vision of the house; everything is connected to the house. 'This is the House of God.' We talk about the family and say, 'Welcome to the family.'

"We encourage people to get into what we call 'life in the family.' Life in the family consists of 'the family circle,' which is much like a physical family where you welcome and incorporate someone into the home. When you have a new child, you welcome that baby into the family. The next phase is to instruct the new members of the family. Then you begin to equip them. In the church it's the same way. We move from a welcome to instruction, and then to equipping, where they learn their spiritual gifts and are helped to get plugged into ministry so they can effectively be a part of the body. The final element is fulfillment. Fulfillment comes when you know you're accomplishing the will of God. It's a sense of, 'Why did God create me?' That's where the Great Commission comes in. We help people take short-term missions trips. This year we'll have over 350 people go on short-term mission trips. So we progress from welcome, to instruction, to equipping, to fulfillment."

David Fisher: "We don't have a small-group ministry. There are, however, a variety of small groups. They're just not organized; I think it's probably better that way. I don't think you can program community. It's either there or it's not. Our people have formed it over time.

"We have several constituencies of people, each of which forms its own community within the church. We have a group of people, ages fifty to eighty, who were in our old facilities on Wooddale Avenue. We call them the Wooddale people. They have formed a community. Several of them are in what they call *koinonia* groups that have been together for twenty-five years. They meet once a week, so they don't have a big agenda—they're just Christian friends to each other. In fact, I married one of the daughters of one set of parents. My wife said, 'The greatest gift my parents ever gave me was their friends.' She said that she had ten mothers, and all of them were going to be at the wedding! That was powerful. It wasn't a program; it was a choice people made to be with each other.

"We have a twenty-something group; they don't want to be called anything. We have a young pastor who is 'sort of' in charge of that and he's forming *koinonia* groups. That generation has seen the older generation in their *koinonia* groups and has said, 'We want community like that.'

"People flow in and out, but when they come into this place they say that everyone seems friendly, just seems like they're family. That has to be formed over a long time in a variety of ways. I don't think you *can* program it."

John Piper: "A few years ago we stood back and asked ourselves, 'Do we really take membership seriously here? Is this just a preaching point that people hang on to?' And we said, 'Look, as a team of elders, we are going to give an account to God some day as to how we shepherd this flock (Hebrews 13:17). Does membership count here? If a marriage breaks up, do we do something or just say, "Well, marriages break up, and we don't have time to deal with that"? Do we discipline people and hold them accountable?' We concluded it really *should* matter.

So we took our church covenant—a good, general covenant that calls for a lifestyle committed to giving, doctrine, attendance, and so on—and then took the following position: 'From here on, we're going to make the church covenant a part of our teaching with new members. We're going to have people sign it because we expect them and us to fulfill its obligationsand if they don't, in a loving way we might get in their faces.'

"To make our commitment serious, I preached five weeks on what it means to be a covenant people. We covenanted with each other to *be* church for each other, and we covenanted with God to be faithful to him. From then on, one Sunday morning a quarter, when new members are welcomed into the church after taking the required classes, we line them all up in front, and I turn the covenant into a series of questions. 'Do you engage to fulfill ...?' And they publicly say, 'I do.' Then I turn back to the people, ask the members to stand (usually it appalls our people how few are actually members), and say, 'Now, do you reaffirm your covenant to be church to these new members?' And they say, 'I do.' Then I ask everybody to stand, and we sing some appropriate song. This church exists by virtue of a covenant, by which we look each other in the face and say, 'I will be church to you.'

"Now practically, because I don't know all the people in the church, we create family through small groups. We are 'us.' We have distinctives and values on Sunday morning, but we know that community is far more than merely a shared vision; it's also being in each other's lives. We really work hard on our small-group life. We have a staff member in charge of small groups, and twice a year we recruit for small groups and hand out a list of our small groups: where they are, what they do, how you can get in touch with them. The elders are all connected with small-group leaders. Finally, once every month, I speak at a special gathering of the small-group leaders. We've tried to up the ante of the significance of small groups.

"Yet it's clear to me at this stage of the game that to be part of a fifteen-hundred-person assembly in the morning and part of a twelve-person group in the evening are not enough for most people to connect. People in the large group are anonymous; they hardly connect with anyone. The twelve-person group is too small, and sometimes these groups don't do well and break up after a year. We decided there needed to be midsize groupings, whose main function is networking. That is, you find someone who lives near you. You find someone in a similar family circumstance or someone with the same job as you. Out of that grows the spontaneous relationships that make for lifelong camaraderie."

Russ Rosser: "Recently we began a Single-Again Moms group, particularly for those who are coming out of abusive situations. I sat for over four hours listening to about twenty women share their stories of how they have had to face abuse in their homes, and it was amazing how quickly that time became well-known throughout the congregation. We equip people to carry on that ministry so that I can be available but not necessarily its focal point.

"We also communicate by teaching a course on caring. We take people whose lives have been broken but who are in the process of healing, bring them together with mature people, and help them learn together how to care for one another, so that as a pastor I'm not doing all the caring. But we're preparing and equipping people, providing for them an atmosphere in a small group so that, as they share their pain and their stories, they begin to mutually care one for the other.

"It also occurs in teaching. I teach a membership class with about fifteen to twenty people. The class might run anywhere from eight weeks to six months, depending on the level of maturity or brokenness in the lives of people. The people bond with each other at that stage, and then we move them on to another environment where they can continue to grow and mature and work through relationships. We keep people in the same group so that they can continue to have some experience in caring for each other. It becomes a continuing community.

"In essence, the church provides for people an opportunity to know God personally. It provides for them an opportunity to feel involved in shepherding, in caring, in loving, and in ministering to the needs of people in the body as well as in the community. It also makes others available to them in the midst of crisis. They see how God can take their brokenness and bring about change that will impact them for the rest of their lives."

Q: How would you describe your leadership style?

Rick Kingham: "I'm very relational. I'm not a great manager, so I have to surround myself with people who can keep details in mind. I'm much more of a strategic visionary and influencer—high influence, based on motivation and relationship. I want much more to help develop a staff, help people to know their place in the body, and then let them do what God has called them to do.

"I believe one of the greatest tragedies in the church today is that we have men and women with incredible leadership gifts just sitting in the pews, and because of a pastor's fear to allow them to lead (because of his own insecurities), we don't use some of the greatest gifts God has placed in the body. We have to be comfortable with letting other people lead."

Russ Rosser: "As an urban leader, one has to adjust to the differing expectations that various ethnic groups have of a leader. People from the Spanish and Portuguese cultures want someone to sit down and eat with them, care for them, interact with them, stand in the marketplace, and spend time with them. The Chinese tend to have a different style of leadership; they want to see consensus in whatever is done. The Hispanic people, on the other hand, look to a pastor to be a benevolent dictator—a caring leader who oftentimes gives direction rather than works for consensus.

"You also need to be able to work with women, particularly in societies that tend to be more matriarchal. So an urban pastor must constantly change his style of leadership in order to begin where people are and then to empower them and equip them."

Joe Stowell: "I am driven by relationships. I need to have a close, good relationship with those I'm leading. When that's threatened or when it's not there, my impulse moves me to repair the relationship before I try to lead any longer. I need to have relationships pretty much in place before I feel confident that I can take this group I'm leading to the next step and to the next place.

"I also like to build consensus. I don't like to be out there saying, 'This is the right thing to do,' and not have people affirm that direction. The important people I trust and believe in have to affirm that it is indeed the right thing to do. I lead with greater power when I have the right people affirming my leadership."

Q: How would you describe your identity as pastor, and where did that identity come from?

Rick Kingham: "I see myself as a shepherd. If you view yourself as a shepherd, several things happen. You recognize you're dealing not with an organization, with a corporate structure (although business work must be done). The pastor must see himself primarily as a shepherd. That keeps him in touch with what I call the 'organic,' a sense of being absolutely and totally dependent on God. If you view yourself as a CEO, you know there must be a plan somewhere that will get this thing done. If you view yourself as a shepherd of sheep, you can't loose yourself from recognizing and acknowledging that God is the Chief Shepherd and that you are an undershepherd of God's sheep. You're not a hireling; you're a shepherd. But God is the Shepherd, and they are *his* sheep, the sheep of his pasture. It keeps you dependent on him.

"If a pastor is secure in who he is, he knows that nobody can take his place. He has something that no one else has, and that is the call of God to lead the people—the call of God to minister, to pastor, and to shepherd God's people. Nobody else has that. Simply because others have wonderful gifts of leadership does not make them a threat."

Russ Rosser: "To be a shepherd, I think one has to be affirmed by the Father in heaven. I've been helped by an article by Henry Nouwen, who wrote 'Moving From Solitude, to Community, to Ministry.'" On the basis of Luke 6:12–20, he pointed out that Jesus found in his communion with the Father all that he needed. When he ministered to the motley crew of twelve, he didn't look for *affirmation* from them; rather, he *ministered* to them. It's out of solitude in your relationship to God and to his affirmation that you move into community and become able to be a buffer in each other's lives. You are then prepared to touch the people who are lost in your community. That will keep you from being blown out of the water."

John Piper: "My sense of calling is radically rooted in my sense of God's purpose for the universe and his creation, as I have seen it through the eyes of Jonathan

Edwards. That is, God created the universe to display his glory, and we display that glory through knowing it truly and cherishing it duly. There's a head-notional component of doctrine and a heart-affectional component of delight and worship. These two together echo back to God his excellence; one's life is changed, and that display of his glory becomes lived out in the world. This model of God's radical God-centeredness governs me entirely, so that I see myself as one who continually lifts up that banner.

"Our vision statement here is also my life's vision statement: 'We exist to spread a passion for the supremacy of God in all things for the joy of all peoples.' That is the mission statement of our church and of my life."

Q: How did you arrive at your current philosophy of ministry?

Glenn Blossom: "One of the great influences for me was working with a man named Dr. Howard Sugden in Lansing, Michigan. He was a pastor of a large church who really gave himself to people. Once a week, even in his older years, he would go to the home of an infirm man and help him. He was always talking about people, naming them. That's something that I try to do.

"My father pastored smaller churches, and he cared about people. My mother was a wonderful pastor's wife; if anyone was called to be a pastor's wife, it was my mother. It was her care for people, visiting and caring."

David Fisher: "Trial and error, theologizing, living, observing. It's still in process. I was writing *The 21st Century Pastor* while serving at another church. I was telling my wife about one of the chapters—I forget which one—and she asked me the question that became the question of my life: 'You're not doing what you're writing about anymore, are you?' she asked. That was part of the reason I left there and came here. I was never going to be a shepherd there."

Q: As a pastor, what do you regard as your most important duty or responsibility?

Glenn Blossom: "The sheep need to be fed well and rightly, so they need a good diet. The sheep need the shepherd's attention. In another sense the pastor must also be a prophet, a priest, and a king. There is a high-priestly role, an intercessory role. A pastor must give priority to prayer, to bear his people before the Lord. I place priority in being with the people."

David Fisher: "Ironically, I think it is to lead the church, because that is what a shepherd does. He takes them from one pasture to another. He doesn't let any strays get away, and he makes sure all of them are safe. Even the feeding of the flock is a leadership function. I don't do that in the form of a strategic plan, though we have people who do that. I'm always thinking, *Where does this congregation need to be, and how can I get them there?*

"My first responsibility is to preach or teach, second is to lead the congregation, and third is to manage the staff to create a team of undershepherds who care for each other, so it becomes a natural thing to care for the flock."

Rick Kingham: "A pastor's primary responsibility is to help his people find God's purpose and plan for their lives and to help them to be fulfilled within the body by being equipped to do the work of the ministry. A pastor does that by creating the atmosphere, by setting the tone, by modeling the example, by providing the critical biblical teaching, and by literally being a father to the people. The Bible says we have a lot of teachers but not many fathers. By being that father, we represent to the body the love of God and the fatherhood of God. We need to allow them to see the transparency, the brokenness, the contriteness, and the humility of a man who is on a journey himself but who understands fully the direction that God wants to take the flock.

"I think my most important duty as pastor is to be on my knees, on my face before the Lord, so I can live as a man of integrity, a man of humility, a man who is contrite, a man who does not abuse his power. I think a pastor must be so connected to the Vine that people can honestly put their lives in his care as a shepherd. They don't have to fear they're going to be led anywhere but where the Lord, our Shepherd, would lead us. And that is by still waters and green pastures."

Chapter 12

·····

THIS WAY TO REVIVAL

·····

What would happen if we turned once more to the Bible's central model for pastors? What would happen in our neighborhoods, our communities, even our nation if pastors took seriously God's call to shepherd the flock of God?

I believe a church led by caring shepherds would provide such a radically appealing vision of human life that our secular, fragmented society couldn't help but clamor to get inside. Could God be withholding his hand of revival until our churches are graced with pastor-shepherds at the helm? I believe he could be—and that is another reason I am so passionate that we rediscover the wisdom of God's shepherd model.

Frankly, I don't think there will be a revival until we have a restoration of pastoral ministry. Without shepherds at the helm, the church isn't prepared to handle revival. I think the church must repent of the mechanisms we have pursued that have created this secularized state we call the church.

WHAT COULD HAPPEN?

What could happen if shepherds once more led the flock of God? How might God be pleased to respond to such a humble step of obedience? I think at least four things would happen.

1. *The Sheep Would Follow.*

When we give our sheep rest and refreshment, instruction, training, and discipline, we provide them with security, loving fellowship, and friendship. And sheep always respond to a caring shepherd.

Of course, every church has its dysfunctional sheep. God says, "Love them anyway." He tells us, "If you are a true shepherd, you will kneel down and take care of their needs. You will wash their filthy hooves." Remember, the Bible calls Jesus the Good Shepherd, not the Good Leader—and he is our chief model.

2. *Authentic Christian Faith Would Return.*

Pollster George Barna often declares that the reason many non-Christians reject our message is not that they disagree with our theology but because our professions of faith ring hollow. We live no differently than they do, so why should they become one of us? They hear our PR pieces about the church being a family, but it feels like a corporation to them. They hear that it's a community, but they see no evidence. They're told the church is a body, but they wonder, *If that's true, why do I feel so ignored and disenfranchised?*

In revival, when the church learns what it means to be the church and begins to live as community, it becomes a powerfully attractive force. It is different from the world in a way that intrigues outsiders; it offers the very thing desperate people are looking for. Genuineness and authenticity always appeal to searching people.

In revivals past, societal change didn't take place because believers picketed offensive businesses or voted out corrupt legislators. The sheer presence of a revived church transforms a sick society.

In the Great Awakening, observers talked about "holiness zones." As an inner circle of Christians listened to Whitefield or some other preacher, the next circle out was often filled with angry men ridiculing, mocking, and throwing rocks at the speaker. Their turf came to be known as a "holiness zone" because when an invitation to accept Christ was given, it was often that very area where hooligans and mockers and roughnecks would be touched by God in remarkable ways. Convicted to the heart by the Spirit of God, they fell down, wailing over their sin, and pleaded with God to save their wretched souls. They thought they were at a safe distance, but suddenly they found themselves in the "holiness zone"—and they came to Christ!

Those who stood in front of Whitefield to protect him from flying projectiles weren't professional bodyguards, just ordinary believers. They had the sense that, "This is us. We will stand together. We will protect our own. It's not someone else's job; it's ours." More than one mocker came to Christ when he saw the reality of the Christian faith of these ordinary Christians who risked their personal safety in order to protect their own.

3. Spontaneous Works of Mercy Would Erupt.

Have you seen the bumper sticker, "Practice random acts of kindness and senseless acts of beauty"? When true revival comes, those words accurately describe the practice of the church. Prayer groups spring up everywhere and believers spontaneously begin to meet the needs of those requiring care. It's always intrigued me that we have to *organize* care for the poor or ministries to bring people to church, when any number of individuals who attend church drive right past those people's homes every day. Revived believers spontaneously look for ways to meet human needs.

4. It Would Become Impossible for Outsiders to Ignore Christ and His Church.

When revival comes to the church, non-Christians are either repulsed by it or they are attracted to it. But they can't ignore it.

I think today's church can easily be ignored. Oh, we've tried not to be ignored through noisy political involvement: "Listen to us, or we'll rally millions of voters and vote you out." "Listen to us, or we'll form our own political party." "Listen to us, or we'll . . ."

The New Testament church, however, did not go in for noisy political activism. The first-century church became a force to be reckoned with because an enormous passion for God drove it. The community of believers protected each other. They lived together, they gave together, they rejoiced together, and they even died together. They hid together in the catacombs. Eventually, their dynamic, growing strength conquered the Roman Empire.

Think about that. This small band of people brought fear to a mighty, brutal empire and could not be ignored, simply because of the zeal of their passion and the strength of their relationships. A Roman general said, "Never have I seen such tenacity of love." He complained that if you killed one, three more would take his or her place.

With an insignificant number of people, the New Testament church overwhelmed a huge military empire. Its success had nothing to do with politics and everything to do with the strength of its character, its community life, its commitment to Christ.

When genuine revival breaks out, such a relational dynamic so fills the community that it either repulses some (who attack it) or compels others to join (who cannot resist it). But the church will not be ignored.

PRAYING FOR REVIVAL

No one can live forever on a mountaintop experience, but it's on the mountaintop that God gives us a taste of something powerful and unique that causes our hearts to long for more. Revival is such a mountaintop experience. That is why thousands of people across this nation are hoping and planning and praying for revival.

Unfortunately, I believe most of them are praying completely amiss.

You see, they're praying for revival so that God will fix our country, so that we will have more Christians in political office, so that kids can pray in our public schools. But very few are praying for revival so that God would give us a holy passion for him. Who is praying for the kind of revival that inspires in us such a vibrant walk of faith that we will fall on our faces before him because we know his real and awesome presence? Most say, "I'm just sick of what's happening in my country, so I'm praying for revival."

Now, don't get me wrong. I believe the church needs revival! It needs to be awakened anew to the heart of God— but not so our lives become easier. The truth is, true revival always brings persecution. Jesus said, "If they persecuted me, they will persecute you also" (John 15:20). Paul added, "In fact, everyone who wants to live a godly life in Christ Jesus will be persecuted" (2 Timothy 3:12). When revival hit Pisidian Antioch, Paul and Barnabas got the boot. When revival hit Lystra and Derbe, Paul's enemies stoned him and left him for dead. When revival came to Corinth, the Jews hauled Paul into court and charged him with heresy. This time Paul escaped physical harm, but an angry mob beat Sosthenes, the local synagogue ruler, right outside the courtroom (Acts 18:17). When eighteenth-century revivalist George Whitefield preached, they threw rocks at him and spit on him; they didn't award him a plaque for Preacher of the Year.

So things could get worse.

And the "worse" could start even in the church. You see, pursuing spiritual passion is a scary thing for most folks. If the pastor has strong gifts and abilities and the church is doing well, it's going to be both difficult and scary for him to assess whether he's really a shepherd. In the corporate world, the bottom line is everything. So if a church seems to be successful, it's pretty hard to say, "We may be growing at a phenomenal rate ... and still be a failure."

Sometimes the challenge to a church's status quo happens like this: Someone comes home from a conference where, for the first time in his life, he's tasted authentic worship. He wants to re-create at his church some of what he experienced at the conference, but he is told, "You have to understand, we don't do that here." So he responds, "Look, I don't have to lift my hands in the service if that's not what we do here. But I *do* have to truly worship God. I must do more than sing a couple of hymns and a couple of choruses and then go home and say I worshiped because I put in an hour and fifteen minutes."

Such a person is not talking about form, but about function. Heaven has inspired many authentic ways of worshiping the one true God. I have been to churches where worship leaders really cranked it up, yet the spirit behind the worship was no different from that in a staid, stone-cold church; both might as well have been buried along with Pompeii in the eruption of Vesuvius. I walked out saying, "Humph. Didn't meet with God. I'm not sure he was even there." The issue is not form, but the reality of a vibrant, personal walk with the living God. Once people have seen and tasted the presence of the Holy One of Israel, nothing else will ever satisfy their heart's deep longing.

IS THERE MORE?

I'm not claiming that everyone in a "corporate" style church is unhappy and unfulfilled. Not every Christian in America is bleeding by the roadside. Many appear to be healthy, productive, and content. But I wonder, Are they experiencing all that God has for them? We might think we're doing fine, but if God has more for us, shouldn't we want it? I don't want to miss out on anything God has for me.

In the final book of *The Chronicles of Narnia*, C. S. Lewis paints a marvelous vision of the afterlife. His heroes have died and have arrived on the outskirts of heaven, a place wonderful beyond description. But the further and deeper they move in, the more real and beautiful and thrilling their new world becomes. As the Faun says to Lucy:

> "The further up and the further in you go, the bigger everything gets. The inside is larger than the outside."
>
> Lucy looked hard at the garden and saw that it was not really a garden at all but a whole world, with its own rivers and woods and sea and mountains. But they were not strange: she knew them all.
>
> "I see," she said. "This is still Narnia, and, more real and more beautiful than the Narnia down below, just as it was more real and more beautiful than the Narnia outside the Stable door! I see . . . world within world, Narnia within Narnia. . . ."
>
> "Yes," said Mr. Tumnus, "like an onion: except that as you continue to go in and in, each circle is larger than the last."[1]

Whatever measure of "success" or fulfillment we have enjoyed by ministering in the way prescribed by an incomplete model, imagine what might lie ahead for us should we choose God's methods and follow God's model instead! Then for us, as for the children of Narnia, it might be "only the beginning of the real story. All their life in this world and all their adventures in Narnia had only been the cover and the title page: now at last they were beginning Chapter One of the Great Story, which no one on earth has read: which goes on forever: in which every chapter is better than the one before."[2]

Or consider a biblical image. Perhaps we may be compared to the twelve "disciples" described in Acts 19. The apostle Paul encountered these men in Ephesus on one of his missionary trips and asked them, "Did you receive the Holy Spirit when you believed?" They answered, "No, we have not even heard that there is a Holy Spirit" (Acts 19:2).

When Paul learned they had received only the baptism of John, he told them of Christ and immediately baptized them into the name of the Lord Jesus. As soon as the apostle placed his hands on them, "the Holy Spirit came on them, and they spoke in tongues and prophesied" (19:6).

Now, these dozen men were having a good time even before Paul came along. There is no indication in the text that they were looking for anything greater. Imagine: They had no idea how much more God wanted to give them!

Could it be we're like those men? By God's grace we may already have experienced grace upon grace in our ministry ... but what if there's more? Good things are happening in many churches, but could even greater things happen with a new commitment to the shepherding perspective? We have some excellent churches, but could they become even greater if they embraced the biblical model? What if the CEO or leadership model were our baptism of John, while the shepherd model were the baptism of Jesus? What more might God have for us if we would endorse and follow the model he gave to his church?

I don't think we are doing all the wrong things, but I do think the reason we're doing them is often wrong, and therefore we're not having the influence we could be enjoying. It certainly isn't wrong to have an evangelistic outreach.

But if we're doing it out of guilt, if we're supporting it out of some misguided sense of obligation, I don't think we please the heart of God. In his sovereignty God may choose to prosper even our errant efforts, but I don't think we best display his heart that way.

While God doesn't always judge methods that do not align with Scripture, he is under no obligation to bless them either. We must ask ourselves, Are we really experiencing his blessing? Is God pleased with us? When outsiders see us, do they see the community of God?

WHAT NOW?

If this message resonates with you, if you think these ideas have something going for them, if you think you need the shepherd model in your church or pastorate—but you're not there now—how do you start turning things around? What do you do now?

My guess is that some of you want to know the precise steps—A, B, C, D—that will show you how to lay it out, how to run it, how to evaluate it, how to make the necessary changes, and how to move things forward. Quite honestly, I'm not sure what to tell you. The model I've spent a book describing is relationally driven. I can't put the whole thing together in a neat, tidy program. I can't write a book that says, "Here are the six steps to be relationally driven."

All I know is, I need to know God more today than I did yesterday. I need to know his people more deeply today than I did yesterday. And that is what will move me into greater effectiveness tomorrow.

In other words, I know the starting point: We must change our mind-set and attitudes, gain a thorough understanding of the church as God's flock, and develop a heart to know God and his people more fully. And then what happens, happens.

I can see that driving a lot of pastors nuts. I can hear them moan, "That's fine, but what am I supposed to *do*?" At

Calvary I talk an awful lot about *being* the church. I say, "Let's get our minds off building the church and talk about more fundamental issues." So we've been asking, What is an authentic Christian? What is spiritual success? What does spiritual passion look like? What are the core values of a church that wants to be the church? How are we to reflect God's nature in the way that we exist and function?

That's not a compelling vision for some; and, in fact, it's much easier to assess successful ministry in the corporate model. It's not hard to say, "We ran these programs and they brought in this many people; we recorded so many professions of faith, received so many new members, and performed so many baptisms." Those things need to happen in any healthy church, of course, but it's not the sum total of ministry. I am not enamored by such numbers, nor am I led to believe the church I have the privilege of shepherding is successful merely because those things are happening at respectable rates.

But what does it mean to assess ministry in the community model? I know the basic ingredients: People are growing closer in their relationship with God and one another; individuals and groups are undergoing transformational change, rather than merely adhering to rules and regulations; and the worshiping community is increasingly experiencing God's grace. But how do you quantify *that*? I know that's what I want, but how do you measure it statistically?

That's a question I'm not sure anyone can answer. How do you answer someone who demands, "Quantify for me how much you love your wife"?

Regardless of how we measure our progress, the starting place for revival is always Scripture. Our first need is to understand the biblical model. This demands a healthy dose of self-examination and self-study.

If you are serious about bringing revival, I encourage you to study what God calls us to be, then begin to preach and teach and interact on what you find. Get off the "doing" kick for a while and focus on questions such as, What are we called to be? What is God's heart for the church? Why does it exist? God didn't have to create the church, so why did he?

Because our people have not, by and large, been taught a sound ecclesiology, if you were to ask the average man or woman in the pew why the church exists, you'd get five answers from three people. Our reason for existence is simply not well understood.

Some believe the church exists to win the lost. That's a great task, but is it really why the church exists? Others say we exist to glorify God and to enjoy him forever. But what does that mean? What does it look like? (Some questions sound almost heretical, but ask them anyway. Truth can take care of itself!)

I agree with those who doubt that the Great Commission is our starting point. In fact, I think when you make the Great Commission the starting point, you actually violate the heart of God. As John Piper has observed, missions exists because worship doesn't.[3] Missions is not the priority; worship is. One day missions will be no more, but worship is forever.

This search for truth might not change everything you do, but it will change why you do what you do, the reasons behind your ministerial activity. And that, in turn, will bring both passion and power to your efforts.

A FEW SUGGESTIONS

God created the church to reflect his image, to be a community that both invites and embraces everyone near it. Authentic community, real family, is enormously attractive, even contagious. There's just something about it that people can't resist!

So how do we begin to communicate that truth, especially if our church is driven by a different commitment? How do we speak to our pastors about this issue?

If you are a layperson in your church, I recommend that you begin to find ways to release your pastor to be a shepherd. Mobilize your gifts as well as the gifts of others to relieve him of some of his current responsibilities so he can be freed to be the shepherd of the sheep. Remove some of the expectations that might now saddle him. If you want to be radical about it, consider putting together a "public ceremony of release" on a Sunday morning. Imagine how freeing it would be for your pastor to have the entire congregation publicly say, "We release you from these expectations and free you to pursue your call to be our shepherd—and, Pastor, here's how we're going to come alongside you in that."

If you are a pastor, it seems to me there are three possible responses to this message: rejoice, repent, or remove yourself.

1. Rejoice.

If your heart beats to the rhythm of a shepherd, if your soul resonates with the picture the Bible paints of a pastor-shepherd, if you long to care for the flock of God, to find the strays, to bind up the wounded, and to love, lead, feed, and care for the Lord's sheep—then rejoice in this role that God has given you and to which he has called you. Rejoice, and keep ministering as you have been.

2. Repent.

If you realize you have pursued the corporate mindset and have acted more as a CEO than as a shepherd, then repent and return to God's way of doing things. Are you guilty of violating God's pattern for those he calls to lead his church? If so, repent, receive the forgiveness God so longs to grant you, and walk in a new way that will please and honor the Lord.

3. Remove Yourself.

If you have concluded that God never called you to pastoral ministry—you've been beating your head against the wall—then, by all means, move quickly to remove yourself from the pastorate. Remove yourself for your own good and for the good of your family and the kingdom of God.

Believe it or not, I don't want this to sound harsh. It's never a failure to find out who we really are. If you are not a pastor, find another way to serve God's people. I talked recently to a graduate of a well-known evangelical seminary who went into the pastorate because that's what his parents wanted him to do. They pushed him to follow the family line. But he was a disaster as a pastor. God never called him to it. He hated it. Finally he left the pastorate, and now he's a businessman in a major city, having the greatest impact of his life. He's leading Bible studies and working with inner-city kids. He and his wife are helping to plant a church—and, man, is he happy!

The church desperately needs pastors with a shepherd's heart. The nation needs churches that ooze community. And the world urgently needs revival—but the church won't know what to do with revival until it is led by shepherds who can bring God's flock to green pastures and cool waters.

UNLEASH THE POWER!

When we pastors stop looking at our people as a herd of cattle to drive but instead see them as members of a family, a flock, bought by the blood of Jesus and in need of care, I believe God will begin to unleash his power and presence on our behalf.

When we begin to show genuine concern and love for the sheep—even to those who are difficult, even to those who keep running in the wrong direction, even to those who cause us great pain—we will again begin to experience God's blessing on our churches, even as God promised so long ago:

> I will give you shepherds after my own heart, who will lead you with knowledge and understanding. (Jeremiah 3:15)

> I will place shepherds over them who will tend them, and they will no longer be afraid or terrified, nor will any be missing. (Jeremiah 23:4)

EPILOGUE:
TIME TO PURSUE SOMETHING ELSE

I personally believe that when the horse dies, it's time to dismount.

Friends, it's time for the church to pursue something else. The executive leader (CEO) model that has captured our fancy simply cannot deliver the goods. God never told us, "Here's a scepter." He said, "Here's a staff." The scepter might look ornate, fancy, and impressive, but God calls us to walk with a staff. We are not royalty; we are servants, shepherds serving under the Great Shepherd.

Others can be kings or priests; others might enjoy the riches of commerce, business, and government. But God's choicest position is that of shepherd, modeled by his Son, taught to his disciples, prophesied to future Israel: "I will give you shepherds after my own heart, who will lead you with knowledge and understanding" (Jeremiah 3:15). This is the pastoral model God chose.

Paul explained all this to the church at Corinth, whose members were debating who had the best pastor, the most effective speaker, the greatest leader. Paul recognized this posturing as an indication of life lived in "the flesh," outside of the power of God, a life that boasted in itself rather than in God. So he reminded this fractious church:

> Brothers, think of what you were when you were called. Not many of you were wise by human standards; not many were influential; not many were of noble birth. But God chose the foolish things of the world to shame

the wise; God chose the weak things of the world to shame the strong. He chose the lowly things of this world and the despised things—and the things that are not—to nullify the things that are, so that no one may boast before him. It is because of him that you are in Christ Jesus, who has become for us wisdom from God—that is, our righteousness, holiness and redemption. Therefore, as it is written, "Let him who boasts boast in the Lord."

When I came to you, brothers, I did not come with eloquence or superior wisdom as I proclaimed to you the testimony about God. For I resolved to know nothing while I was with you except Jesus Christ and him crucified. I came to you in weakness and fear, and with much trembling. My message and my preaching were not with wise and persuasive words, but with a demonstration of the Spirit's power, so that your faith might not rest on men's wisdom, but on God's power. (1 Corinthians 1:26–2:5)

So then, no more boasting about men! All things are yours, whether Paul or Apollos or Cephas or the world or life or death or the present or the future—all are yours, and you are of Christ, and Christ is of God. (1 Corinthians 3:21–23)

It's all of God. Humans can boast no wisdom, no power, nothing of eternal worth. It's all of God. Therefore, the role of shepherd as defined by God, exemplified by Jesus, and foreseen by the prophets, was divinely chosen in order for us to live and breathe as "spiritual" people (1 Corinthians 3:1).

Dependence on God is a prerequisite to securing the understanding, perspective, and allegiance that goes with the pastoral tasks. Only in the absence of the flesh can a pastor draw on the wisdom and power of God. It requires a humbling, an emptying of oneself, a commitment to learning the paths of righteousness in a life lived in total reliance on God.

Access to the power of God through the work of the Holy Spirit is linked directly to the role one assumes before God as a pastoring shepherd, "that no one may boast before him" (1 Corinthians 1:29). The love that a pastor develops for others, exemplified in a shepherd's care, derives directly from his love of God. God specified the shepherd's role in order to develop the shepherd's heart.

God calls pastors to be shepherds. It is not an option, not an entry-level position for career development. It is the defined role that will enable a person of God to develop a heart for God, to learn to experience the power and provision of God, and to properly love and care for the sheep.

But it's hard. It goes against the flesh. It requires resolute focus and commitment. It is the path least traveled, but it is the path dictated by God.

I wince every time I read Charles Jefferson's words, but I admit he hit the nail on the head when he wrote back in 1912, "The shepherd's work is a humble work; such it has been from the beginning and such it must be to the end. A man must come down to it. A shepherd cannot shine. He cannot cut a figure. His work must be done in obscurity...."[1]

It is exactly those kinds of shepherds for whom God continues to search even today. Will you lay down the scepter and pick up the staff? God wants to pour out his blessing on faithful shepherds so that his flock can grow strong and begin to thrive once more.

Will you be one of them?

NOTES

Introduction: Why I Wrote This Book

1. Selected statistics were taken from David Bryant, *The Hope at Hand: National and World Revival for the Twenty-First Century* (Grand Rapids: Baker, 1995).

Chapter 1: The Church, Inc.

1. George Barna, *The Second Coming of the Church* (Nashville: Word, 1998), 1; all rights reserved.

2. For ease of reading, throughout this book I will be using masculine singular pronouns for the pastor rather either the plural or the awkward "he/she," "his/her," etc.

3. Ken Garfield, "Myers Park Pastor Resigns As Church 'CEO,'" *The Charlotte Observer*, January 14, 1999, 1C, 4C.

4. Barna, *The Second Coming of the Church*, 8; all rights reserved.

5. Ibid.; all rights reserved.

Chapter 2: The Neglected Model

1. Charles Edward Jefferson, *The Minister As Shepherd* (New York: Thomas Y. Crowell, 1912), 7–8, 10. A revised edition of this book is now available from Christian Literature Crusade, Fort Washington, Pa., 1998.

2. Ibid., 12.

3. Ibid., 17.

4. Ibid., 19–20.

5. R. Laird Harris, Gleason L. Archer Jr., and Bruce K. Waltke, eds., *Theological Wordbook of the Old Testament* (Chicago: Moody, 1980), 853.

6. Ibid., 121.

7. Francis Brown, S. R. Driver, and Charles A. Briggs, *The New Brown, Driver, and Briggs Hebrew and English Lexicon of the Old Testament* (Lafayette, Ind.: Associated Publishers and Authors, 1907; reprint 1981), 129.

8. Harris, Archer, and Waltke, *Theological Wordbook of the Old Testament*, 731.

9. Brown, Driver, and Briggs, *Hebrew and English Lexicon of the Old Testament*, 1073.

10. Harris, Archer, and Waltke, *Theological Wordbook of the Old Testament*, 977.

11. Ibid., 852.

12. Ibid., 853.

13. Ralph Alexander, "Ezekiel," in *The Expositor's Bible Commentary*, ed. Frank E. Gaebelein (Grand Rapids: Zondervan, 1986), 6:912.

14. David Fisher, *The 21st Century Pastor* (Grand Rapids: Zondervan, 1996), 213.

15. Jefferson, *The Minister As Shepherd*, 30–31.

16. Ibid., 35–36.

17. Ibid., 22–23.

18. Ibid., 42.

Chapter 3: A Disastrous Shift

1. David Fisher, *The 21st Century Pastor* (Grand Rapids: Zondervan, 1996), 9.

2. Thomas C. Oden, *Pastoral Theology* (San Francisco: Harper & Row, 1982), viii.

3. Ibid., xii.

4. Seward Hiltner, *Preface to Pastoral Theology* (Nashville: Abingdon, 1958), 15.

5. Fisher, *The 21st Century Pastor*, 10.

6. Jay E. Adams, *Shepherding God's Flock*, vol. 1, *The Pastoral Life* (Philadelphia: Presbyterian and Reformed, 1975), 1.

7. Fisher, *The 21st Century Pastor*, 41.

8. John Piper, *The Supremacy of God in Preaching* (Grand Rapids: Baker, 1990). What's the object of preaching from the Bible at all, if it's all raw pragmatism? Just to help our audience feel better? I don't think so. As Jay Adams said years ago: "If the Spirit of God is convicting them, what am I doing helping them to feel better?"

9. George Barna, *The Second Coming of the Church* (Nashville: Word, 1998), 7; all rights reserved.

10. Quoted in Joseph M. Stowell, *Shepherding the Church* (Chicago: Moody, 1997), 38; used by permission.

11. Fisher, *The 21st Century Pastor*, 76–77.

12. Ibid., 78.

13. Stowell, *Shepherding the Church*, 41; used by permission.

14. Fisher, *The 21st Century Pastor*, 27.

15. Ibid., 41.

16. Hiltner, *Preface to Pastoral Theology*, 15.

17. Ibid., 20.

18. Ibid., 18.

19. Oden, *Pastoral Theology*, x, xi.

Chapter 4: It's Not Rocket Science

1. Joseph D. Korman, from
http://home.earthlink.net/~joekor/rocketscience.htm.

Chapter 5: Who Am I?

1. David Fisher, *The 21st Century Pastor* (Grand Rapids: Zondervan, 1996), 23.

2. Ibid., 27.

3. For "elders," see Acts 11:30; 14:23; 20:17; 1 Timothy 5:17; Titus 1:5; and 1 Peter 5:1. "Overseers" appears in Acts

20:28; 1 Timothy 3:1–2; Titus 1:7; and 1 Peter 5:2; while "teachers" is used in Acts 13:1; 1 Corinthians 12:28; Ephesians 4:11; Hebrews 5:12; and James 3:1. For "prophets," see Acts 11:27; 13:1; 15:32; 1 Corinthians 12:28; and Ephesians 2:20. For "leaders," see Acts 15:22; Galatians 2:2; and Hebrews 13:7, 17, 24.

4. See 2 Timothy 2:4–6.

5. See Galatians 2:9.

6. See William Barclay, *The Gospel of Luke*, rev. ed. (Philadelphia: Westminister, 1975), 22.

Chapter 6: God's Portrait of a Shepherd

1. Lynn Anderson, *They Smell Like Sheep* (West Monroe, La.: Howard Publishing, 1997), 11–12.

2. Jay E. Adams, *Shepherding God's Flock*, vol. 1, *The Pastoral Life* (Philadelphia: Presbyterian and Reformed, 1975), 5.

3. William Barclay, *The Gospel of John*, vol. 2 (Daily Study Bible; Philadelphia: Westminster, 1975), 55.

4. See Hebrews 1:3; Philippians 2:6; 2 Corinthians 4:4; and John 14:9.

5. Barclay, *The Gospel of John*, 52.

6. Ibid., 53.

7. Ibid.

8. Ibid., 54–55.

9. Joseph M. Stowell, *Shepherding the Church* (Chicago: Moody, 1997), 185; used by permission.

10. Ibid., 180; used by permission.

Chapter 7: Leader or Shepherd?

1. George Barna, *The Second Coming of the Church* (Nashville: Word, 1998), 99; all rights reserved for quotes from this book in this chapter.

2. Ibid., 198.

3. Ibid., 202–3.

4. Ibid., x.

5. Ibid., 210.

6. Ibid., 101.

7. Ibid., 106.

8. Ibid., 107.

9. Ibid., 31.

10. Ibid., 96.

11. Joseph M. Stowell, *Shepherding the Church* (Chicago: Moody, 1997), 187; used by permission.

12. Jay E. Adams, *Shepherding God's Flock*, vol. 1, *The Pastoral Life* (Philadelphia: Presbyterian and Reformed, 1975), 9.

13. See David Bennett, *Metaphors of Ministry* (Grand Rapids: Baker, 1993).

Chapter 8: The Call of God

1. C. E. Colton, *The Minister's Mission* (Grand Rapids: Zondervan, 1951), 14.

2. Charles U. Wagner, *The Pastor: His Life and Work* (Schaumburg, Ill.: Regular Baptist Press, 1976), 13.

3. Jack W. Hayford, *Pastors of Promise* (Ventura, Calif.: Regal, 1997), 20.

4. Wagner, *The Pastor: His Life and Work*, 13.

5. Joseph M. Stowell, *Shepherding the Church* (Chicago: Moody, 1997), 80; used by permission.

6. Jay E. Adams, *Shepherding God's Flock*, vol. 1, *The Pastoral Life* (Philadelphia: Presbyterian and Reformed, 1975), 7.

7. Os Guinness, *The Call* (Nashville: Word, 1998), 29.

8. Charles H. Spurgeon, *Lectures to My Students*, condensed and abridged by David Otis Fuller (Grand Rapids: Zondervan, 1945), 30–31.

9. William Bauer, William F. Arndt, F. Wilbur Gingrich, and Frederick W. Danker, *A Greek-English Lexicon of the New Testament and Other Early Christian Literature*, 2d ed. (Chicago: Univ. of Chicago Press, 1979), 579.

10. Ibid., 293.

11. Ibid., 766.

12. Ibid., 706.

13. Erwin W. Lutzer, *Pastor to Pastor: Tackling Problems of the Pulpit* (Chicago: Moody, 1987), 11.

14. John Jowett, *The Preacher, His Life and Work* (Grand Rapids: Baker, 1968 [repr.]), 21.

15. Charles Bridges, *The Christian Ministry: With an Inquiry Into the Causes of Its Inefficiency* (Carlisle, Pa.: Banner of Truth, 1997), 90.

16. Lutzer, *Pastor to Pastor*, 11.

17. Jowett, *The Preacher, His Life and Work*, 12.

18. Lutzer, *Pastor to Pastor*, 10.

19. Richard Baxter, *The Reformed Pastor: A Pattern for Personal Growth and Ministry*, abridged and edited by James M. Houston (Portland, Ore.: Multnomah, 1982), 68.

20. Henlee H. Barnette, *Christian Calling and Vocation* (Grand Rapids: Baker, 1965), 80.

Chapter 9: The Glory of Shepherds

1. Jack W. Hayford, *Pastors of Promise* (Ventura, Calif.: Regal, 1997), 20.

2. Ibid., 21.

3. Ibid., 21–22.

4. Charles H. Spurgeon, *Lectures to My Students*, condensed and abridged by David Otis Fuller (Grand Rapids: Zondervan, 1945), 39.

Chapter 10: Connected, Relational Ministry

1. See, for example, John 13:34–35; Romans 12:10, 16; 13:8; 14:13; 15:7, 14; 16:16; 2 Corinthians 13:12; Galatians 5:13; Ephesians 4:2, 32; 5:19, 21; Colossians 3:13, 16; 1 Thessalonians 5:11; Hebrews 3:13; 10:24, 25; James 4:11; 1 Peter 1:22; 3:8; 4:9; 5:5, 14; 1 John 1:7; 3:11, 23; 4:7, 11, 12; 2 John 5.

2. Lewis Sperry Chafer, *Major Bible Themes*, revised by John F. Walvoord (Grand Rapids: Zondervan, 1974), 237.

3. Jonathan Edwards, "An Essay on the Trinity," *Treatises on Grace and Other Posthumously Published Writings*, ed. Paul Helm (Cambridge: James Clarke, 1971), 108.

4. Ibid., 118.

5. John Piper, *The Pleasures of God* (Portland, Ore.: Multnomah, 1991), 40.

6. John Piper, *Living by Faith in Future Grace: The Purifying Powers of Living by Faith* (Sisters, Ore.: Multnomah, 1995), 31ff.

7. This was the subject of my last book, *The Heart of a Godly Man: Practical Disciplines for a Man's Spiritual Life* (Chicago: Moody, 1997).

Chapter 11: But Does It Work?

1. The telephone interviews took place on the following dates: Joseph Stowell, December 11, 1998; Rick Kingham, December 11, 1998; Glenn Blossom, December 12, 1998; John Piper, December 14, 1998; David Fisher, December 15, 1998; and Russ Rosser, December 18, 1998.

Chapter 12: This Way to Revival

1. C. S. Lewis, *The Last Battle* (New York: Collier, 1956), 180.

2. Ibid., 184.

3. See John Piper, *Let the Nations Be Glad! The Supremacy of God in Missions* (Grand Rapids: Baker, 1993).

Epilogue: Time to Pursue Something Else

1. Charles Edward Jefferson, *The Minister As Shepherd* (New York: Thomas Y. Crowell, 1912), 35.